WHY ARE WE HERE?

Teachings of
The Order of Christian Mystics

WHY ARE WE HERE?

Teachings of The Order of Christian Mystics
The "Curtiss Books" freely available at
www.orderofchristianmystics.co.za

1. The Voice of Isis
2. The Message of Aquaria
3. The Inner Radiance
4. Realms of the Living Dead
5. Coming World Changes
6. The Key to the Universe
7. The Key of Destiny
8. Letters from the Teacher Volume I
9. Letters from the Teacher Volume II
10. The Truth about Evolution and the Bible
11. The Philosophy of War
12. Personal Survival
13. The Pattern Life
14. Four-Fold Health
15. Vitamins
16. Why Are We Here?
17. Reincarnation
18. For Young Souls
19. Gems of Mysticism
20. The Temple of Silence
21. The Divine Mother
22. The Soundless Sound
23. The Mystic Life
24. The Love of Rabiacca
25. Potent Prayers

Supporting Volumes

26. The Seventh Seal
27. Towards the Light

WHY ARE WE HERE?

AND OTHER ESSAYS ON
Cosmic Soul Science

Transcribed by
HARRIETTE AUGUSTA CURTISS
and
F. HOMER CURTISS, B.S., M.D.
Founders of
THE ORDER OF CHRISTIAN MYSTICS
and
AUTHORS OF THE "CURTISS BOOKS"

2014 EDITION

REPUBLISHED FOR THE ORDER BY
MOUNT LINDEN PUBLISHING
JOHANNESBURG, SOUTH AFRICA
ISBN: 978-1-920483-00-5

"Ministers of Christ and Stewards of the Mysteries of God."
1 Corinthians 4 vs. 1

COPYRIGHT 2014

BY
MOUNT LINDEN PUBLISHING

First Published in 1941

May be used for non-commercial, personal, research and educational use.
ALL RIGHTS RESERVED

TABLE OF CONTENTS

CHAPTER		PAGE
I	Why Are We Here?.	1
II	The Object of Physical Existence.	9
III	New Dimensions.	26
IV	With Courage and Faith.	35
V	Old Clothes.	43
VI	Ideals.	54
VII	The Woman's Age.	63
VIII	Smile, Smile, Smile.	75
IX	The Cloud Upon the Mountain.	90
X	All Conquering Love.	103
XI	The Heaven World.	115
XII	Christ in the Daily Life.	131

FOREWORD

If a number of persons were viewing a large diamond suspended above the heads of the group, and were asked to name its color, each might give a different answer. One might say it was red. Another might say it was blue, another green or orange or yellow or any other color. They might each check the report of their senses with a spectroscope and scientifically prove their report to be true. They might fight to the death to maintain the truth of their view. And they all might be right, viewed from their standpoint on the Plane of Manifestation, the plane of differentiation.

But if they all rose above the diamond, they would see that it had no color, but was white. The colors they saw were only differentiated aspects of the one white light. Hence the truths for which they fought were only relative truths, varied according to their point of view on the Plane of Manifestation.

Just so is it with other truths in the intellectual as well as in the physical world. Really to understand them we must get above the Plane of Manifestation to the Plane of Causation. We need not necessarily give up our old concepts, but merely recognize their limitations and relative truth and importance, and then expand them. Then we will not be misled by appearances or by acute and outstanding symptoms.

The cause of a disease may be simple in itself but may have many symptoms. To abolish all the symptoms we must first recognize the cause and eliminate it. In fact, all great things are simple in essence, altho often difficult to explain because manifold in expression on the Plane of Manifestation. Therefore, to grasp the essential truth of a concept we must view it from the Plane of Causation and thus get the Cosmic Concept of it. It is this Cosmic Concept of Truth and Life which we have tried to express in these essays on Cosmic Soul Science.

THE AUTHOR

Washington, D. C.
1941.

CHAPTER I

WHY ARE WE HERE?

The Problem:

The origin and destiny of man is one of the greatest philosophical problems that has occupied the mind of man. And it has occupied the finest minds of all races throughout all ages. And it still is one of the most important problems for mankind to understand; for without some comprehension of why we find ourselves occupying a physical body and manifesting here on Earth, and apparently without our having been consulted, life has no meaning, has no reason or explanation, and especially has no definite objective toward the attainment of which our efforts should be directed.

Unsolved by Science:

To the great mass of mankind the reason for life here on Earth is still as great a mystery today as ever it was in the Dark Ages, in spite of the great advances in science and invention and our so-called modern, streamlined civilization. One reason why science has not solved this great problem is that science does not deal with original causes; only with their effects. It does not deal with ultimate origins; only with their manifested phenomena.

All From the Unseen:

Since all the manifested universe comes from the unseen and the intangible into the seen and the tangible, the source of causation must lie far above the plane of its materialization, the plane of physics, or matter and its measurable effects. Physical science therefore deliberately shuts itself off from the study of ultimate origins, saying that they belong not in the realm of physics, but of metaphysics and philosophy. Science, therefore, does not pretend to study life itself; only the phenomena which life exhibits as it manifests on Earth through the various forms which we call living things.

Problem Not Insoluble:

But the origin of life and consciousness was not an insoluble problem to the ancient sages and philosophers, nor even to the modern mystics, because they looked behind the phenomena to the noumenon; back of the material manifestation to the immaterial thing-in-itself or the invisible cause of the manifestation. And having once grasped the Law of Causation and Manifestation they saw it illustrated and exemplified on every hand, as we all can do.

Nothing Happens: (First fundamental concept)

Since this great cosmic problem and philosophical mystery is so comprehensive in its sweep, in order to bring it within the scope of our essay we will call your attention to, and ask you to keep clearly in mind, only three fundamental concepts. The first concept that we should realize is that *nothing happens*. Everything manifests according to the Law of Cause and Effect; according to law and order.

Plan, Purpose and Design:

Everywhere in Nature around us we see plan, purpose, design and the will to manifest, from the geometrical form of the snowflake to the formation of a solar system or a universe. For instance, there is no little oak tree in the acorn, and yet the acorn invariably unfolds according to, and materializes, the plan or invisible pattern of the oak and no other kind of tree. Why? There is no little bird within the egg, and yet from the egg of each species of bird, that particular kind of bird, and no other, emerges. Why?

Evolution From Within:

From a spiral nebula a solar system with its suns, moons and planets appears. Why? From the single cell of a fertilized ovum the body of man appears. Why? Out of an inchoate Chaos an orderly Cosmos evolves, not haphazardly but evidently according to plan, purpose and design. In other words, everything that we see in the manifested universe around us has already existed in itself in the super-physical worlds before it was materialized.

Physical Appearance Temporary:

Therefore, everything appears from out the unseen according to the plan for its aspect of divine manifestation which already existed in the invisible Worlds of Causation. Its physical expression is but a temporary and partial manifestation or materialization of the thing-in-itself for a brief cycle here in the realm of matter.

The Grand Plan:

And this takes place according to a conscious plan, purpose and design, and will to manifest. Back of the whole universe, therefore, there must be a Grand Plan in which every manifestation occupies its appointed place.

Pre-existence:

This doctrine of the pre-existence of all things before their physical manifestations is illustrated in many biblical passages. Not only was "every plant of the field *before* it was in the earth, and every herb *before* it grew," but, "Verily, verily I say unto you, *Before* Abraham was, I am."[1] "And now, O Father, glorify thou me with thine

---
[1] *St. John*, viii, 58.

own self with the glory which I had with thee *before the world was*. . . . For thou lovedst me *before the foundations* of the world."[2] And this same doctrine is the basis of all great religions and is implicit in most philosophies.

Chicken or Egg?

It also answers the ancient conundrum; Which came first, the chicken or the egg? Naturally the egg came first. In answer to the question as to where the first egg came from, we need only point out that all living things manifest on Earth through the agency of an egg of some kind, a germ-cell or seed.

Primary Pattern:

The original egg or seed of each species of life is precipitated and materialized out of the invisible as an expression in embryo of the concept, ideal, thought-form or archetype of each species of plant, animal or other form of life which is projected from the Divine Mind for expression in the worlds of form. The egg or seed thus materialized acts as a focal point on Earth through which the constructive and cohesive currents of the One Life of God materializes the invisible pattern of that which is to be manifested on Earth.

Man not Insignificant:

Since man is an integral part of the universe and of Nature, we must assume that he too has his particular place in the Grand Plan of the Universe through which God expresses Himself in all worlds. In fact, each of us has and occupies a definite place and fulfills a definite function in that Grand Plan. Far from man's being but an infinitesimal speck of life on one of the smallest planets of a minor solar system, he is a vitally important factor in the whole great scheme of the manifested universe. For

---

[2] *St. John*, xvii, 5-24.

without each individual Soul's functioning in his own place, *the whole Grand Plan would be imperfect* to that extent, and to that extent God Himself would find imperfect expression in all the worlds of manifestation.

The Real Man:

The Real man, therefore, exists *independent of* and *prior to his physical embodiment*, as a result of causes and purposes far beyond and superior to his appearance on Earth. Hence, if we are intelligently to co-operate with the great Law of Manifestation and worthily occupy our place and accomplish our part in the Grand Plan, we must know something of our origin and destiny, or the object of physical existence.

Man not a Mortal: (Second fundamental concept)

Realization of the first great concept of the pre-existence of all things naturally implies the second fundamental principle, namely, that *man is not a mortal*, that is, subject to death. This may be a startling statement to some at first thought, but a little reflection will show that we are not even entirely human! We all recognize that a part of us is animal: and yet not a part of us, but only the physical instrument through which man, the Real Self, expresses himself on Earth. While part of our expression, the physical instrument, is animal, a part is also human; that is, the personal aspect of our individualized minds. But just as the body is not the Real Man, neither is the mind the pre-existing Real Man.

Mind an Instrument:

Mind is only the mental instrument through which the consciousness of the Real Man finds expression through the formation of concrete ideas and their resulting thought-forms in the mental world, which thought-forms, in turn, find expression through the mechanism of the brain. Man is, therefore, not a mortal because he is neither merely a human-animal nor its personal mind, nor does he cease to exist when he withdraws from his physical instrument at so-called death.

The Spiritual Being:

The Real Man is essentially a divine, Spiritual Being, an emanation of the universal Causeless Cause, an individualized Ray of that universal Cosmic Spirit which men call God. Man is not a mortal possessing a Soul, but is an immortal Soul striving for expression through a mortal organism.

Immortality:

All manifested things on the Earth-plane have a beginning and an end, but not the Real Self. For we are immortal beings here and now, utilizing both our bodies and our minds as instruments through which our consciousness can find expression on Earth. *Immortality is not something to be attained, but something inherent*, an embodied phase of which we are all striving to express. The Real Self, therefore, is a Spiritual Being who exists quite independent of and far superior to its limited manifestation through the human-animal personality.

The Earth not our Home: (Third fundamental concept)

The third fundamental concept which we should hold in mind is that *this physical world is not our home*. We are only visiting here for a brief span of some three-score years and ten, more or less. This is one of the fundamental concepts back of all religions, since they all teach that we ultimately return to the higher invisible worlds or the spiritual home whence we came. From this realization that the body is not our Real Self and that this Earth-plane is not our home, some sects have apparently jumped to the conclusion that the object of life is to get away from life.

Mastery of the Body:

Because they find that the body is a mortal like any other animal's and therefore gives us considerable trouble until we have trained it to respond to our guidance, they seek to subdue it by asceticism, mortification of the flesh, extreme fasting, emasculation and abuse. But control of organs, functions and desires through weakness and depletion is not mastery; only emasculation. To be a perfect instrument the body should have all its organs and functions in their most nearly perfect normal development, but mastered and controlled.

Asceticism:

Such sects also strive to get away from responsibilities and retreat from life in the world by retiring into the forest, the jungle, the mountains, the monastery or the convent. But the above mentioned realization that the body is not our Real Self and the world is not our real home should teach us not to despise the body nor long to get away from life; for realization is only the first step toward manifestation, while expression is the essence of the Law of Manifestation.

The Aim of Life:

As practical students of the Cosmic School of philosophy, we look upon these problems from just the opposite viewpoint. From our standpoint the highest aim in life is not to get away from life; else why come down to Earth and incarnate at all? We should not seek to get away from life, but to *live life*; to live life *fully and harmoniously and joyously* right in the environment where we find ourselves incarnated; in fact, where we have chosen to incarnate. And we should live our life happily and joyously because of our higher conception of the object of life, and thereby advance to a higher expression of our Real Self.

Living Life:

By "living life to its fullest" we do not mean that we should indulge every appetite and desire of the flesh, for that would be living merely like animals. Neither should we live merely to indulge the whims, vanities, selfishness and petty ambitions of the personality. We should neither kill out nor give free rein to the functions of the animal nor to the desires of the personality, but should *master them all* and *utilize them all* to the glory of God, each in its proper place and for its highest purpose. We will then live life, not as animals, not even as mere human beings, but as Spiritual Beings temporarily seeking expression through the human-animal personality.

Why the Soul Incarnates:

Some may wonder, if the Soul is an individualized Spiritual Being, an immortal Ray of the Divine,—all-perfect, all-wise and all-powerful in its own spiritual realm or home,—why should it come down from its super-dimensional realms into the great limitations necessarily imposed upon it by this three dimensional world of dense, inert physical matter?

CHAPTER II

THE OBJECT OF PHYSICAL EXISTENCE

The Law of Materialization:

It is an axiom of our Cosmic Philosophy that *everything comes from the unseen*, from the abstract to the concrete. "These abstractions become more concrete as they approach our plane of existence, until finally they phenomenalize in the form of the material Universe, by a process of conversion, analogous to that by which steam can be condensed into water, and water frozen into ice."[1] Man appears upon Earth according to this same universal Law of Manifestation or Materialization. But just *why he should do so* is the great problem we are trying to solve.

The Cycle of Necessity:

The answer is that once the Ray of the Spiritual Self is individualized and sent forth from the heart of the Father into the worlds of form on its great outgoing Cycle of Necessity, it must manifest its divinity in all those worlds, including the physical. In other words, the Soul comes down into the limitations of physical embodiment that it may learn to express as much of its divine life, its divine love and its divine consciousness and power here on Earth as it does in heaven.

Incarnation Necessary:

In each incarnation it manifests as much of Itself as it has learned to express through the experiences of its

---

[1] *The Secret Doctrine*, Blavatsky, i, 76.

many previous incarnations, until it finally fully accomplishes its great mission of manifesting its individualized aspect of God here on Earth.

Three Objects:

Besides gradually (a) expressing our inherent Divinity here on earth through (b) learning the lessons which only embodiment in the limitations of physical matter could teach us, there is a third object for our embodiment here in Earth. That is (c) the spiritualization of matter through the spiritual radio-activity of the spiritual forces we allow to flow through the matter composing our bodies and radiate outward to all we contact.

Spiritualizing Matter:

Since man is a Spiritual Being, the radiations of both his consciousness and his spiritual body have a far higher rate of vibration than the matter composing his physical body. Hence, all the matter composing his bodies receives the radionic impress of the spiritual rate he is expressing, and so is raised to a higher rate and tends to be spiritualized to that degree. Thus does man uplift or degrade everything he contacts according to whether his vibrations are spiritual and constructive or whether he has lowered them to destructive rates.

"I Came Down From Heaven":

Jesus explained this great mystery in a few words when He said, speaking of the Christ-consciousness[2] within each heart: "I came down from heaven not to do mine own will, but the will of him that sent me."[3] Now if this is a statement of fact and not theory or speculation; if it is an essential factor in the great Law of Manifestation, then

---

[2] As used in this volume, the term "Christ" refers to the Universal Christ Principle or the individualised Ray of God within each heart. This Ray is often called the Spiritual Self, the Real Self, the Higher Self, the I Am Presence, the God-within, the Christ-within, etc.

[3] *St. John*, vi, 38.

we should find some other expressions of this same factor already worked out in Nature around us. For *the Law is one*, although it finds various expressions on each plane. And if we cannot find such an expression then there is some mistake in the concept of our premise. Therefore, let us see if we can find an example of this Law worked out in Nature around us.

Whence the Oak?

Reverting to the acorn as an illustration, is the acorn materialized out of the invisible and then unfolded into the towering oak just to do its own will or please itself? We can easily imagine that the acorn might be quite content and well satisfied to remain an acorn. It finds itself surrounded by a nice shiny, polished brown shell which is so strong as to protect it from the harsh conditions of the rock and soil and the other dangers of the outer world around it. It is "varnished" outside to protect it from moisture, and it is lined with a soft brown down which keeps it warm and makes it comfortable all during the winter. Then why should it desire to change its present satisfactory form of existence? Its own will would, therefore, naturally be to remain as it is and continue its present comfortable condition of life.

Superior Laws:

But the acorn is subject to forces outside of, and superior to, itself and incomprehensible to its limited aspect of consciousness. When certain greater cycles of life roll around; when the great outpouring of cosmic life on Earth takes place in the Spring, the acorn finds itself subjected to new and unexpected and overwhelming forces quite different from anything it had ever experienced during all its existence. Great and revolutionary changes are taking place both without and within itself. The shiny, varnished shell which formerly protected it from moisture now begins to soften and become pervious to water. And as the water is absorbed the kernel begins to swell and perhaps causes the acorn great suffering from the internal pressure thus produced. And the acorn may say to itself: "The pressure of affairs is getting too great for me. I cannot stand it. I must find some relief or I shall burst."

The Acorn's Tragedy:

The incomprehensible forces which cause it to expand and produce this pressure ultimately reach a crisis, and at last its beautiful protective shell does burst, is split asunder and ruined, and finally disappears, completely absorbed by the new manifestation of the acorn's life. This must seem like a great and appalling catastrophe to the acorn, and therefore not at all in accordance with its own will and desire. Yet how could it realize that it did not come down to Earth to do its own will, but the will of a far greater power than its own personality, the will of Him that sent it into manifestation?

The Sprout Appears:

Then the acorn finds that the dainty germinal sprout which it had so carefully guarded and protected between its two thick starchy cotyledons is being pushed out of its snug warm nest into the cold, harsh conditions of the soil surrounding it. The delicate sprout is being cruelly forced up through the soil by an overwhelming power whether it wants to or not. But, following not its own will but the will of Him that sent it, the acorn continues to push its sprout upward and its rootlets downward, and thus, according to the slow law of growth, a little at a time, or cell by cell, it gradually absorbs from the soil around it just those particular chemical elements and forces which are needed and which must be built into the meshes of its invisible pattern to materialize that pattern as the physical tree.

The New World:

Thus ultimately the sprout pushes up above the soil into an entirely new world, a world of freedom from the darkness and the hard and hampering conditions and oppression of the soil, a world of sunlight and warmth and air of which it could have no possible conception during its earlier stages of growth while encased in its shell or while pushing through the darkness of earth. Then it realizes that it was the unfolding power of the life-force from within that was pushing it outward, and the attractive force of the Sun that was pulling it upward all the time, even though it could not possibly conceive of the end to be attained nor the reasons why, nor the methods and mechanism used.

Gradual Materialization:

The above simple illustration shows that, according to the Law of Manifestation, the gradual materialization of the pre-existing inner pattern here in Earth conditions, each form doing not its own will but the will of Him that sent it, *is a basic law of the manifested universe*. And man, being a part of Nature, must follow the same law.

Our Outer Shell:

We incarnate here on Earth with our Real or Spiritual Self embedded in the soil of the human personality almost as latent and unmanifested as the pattern of the oak is embedded within the acorn. And often for years there seems to be little or no interest in spiritual things and no spiritual unfoldment. During this spiritually dormant stage we are quite content to live within the shell or environment with which we find ourselves surrounded, the shell of the outer life—business, social, intellectual, material—largely limited and influenced by the environment and by the ideas of those with whom we associate, and with no more conception of the worlds of spiritual light and air and freedom which surround us than the acorn has of the world of sunlight and air.

Spiritual Springtime:

But when a certain cycle in our unfoldment dawns, our spiritual springtime, we find ourselves subjected to incomprehensible forces, and a change begins to come over us. Whether we understand it or not or even realize that it is taking place, we begin to respond to the warmth of the Sun of Righteousness and to absorb the waters of Divine Love. Then our hearts begin to soften, our consciousness begins to expand and great pressure is brought to bear on the conditions of our environment.

Our Expanding Consciousness:

Things with which we were content before, now seem inadequate, even hampering. We can no longer get the same pleasure out of the old pursuits and amusements. Old orthodox ideas and conceptions no longer satisfy our expanding consciousness. Old habits of body, of mind, of speech, even the old circle of friends, are outgrown. We may even leave the home-circle and go to some distant place where conditions are so different that it is almost like a new incarnation.

Mental Unrest:

At first the pressure of this inner growth may be so intense as to cause much mental unrest and even suffering, especially if, from force of habit and lack of understanding, and *because of the opinion of others*, we try to cling to the outgrown husks of our former life, habits and conceptions. But ultimately the time comes when the old conditions are at an end and seem to crash down around us and we think our life is ruined. But it is only the breakup of the husks of old conditions that the new growth may manifest. Thus at last we do break through the limitations and bondage of old thoughts and conditions and environment and begin to grow spiritually.

Trials and Troubles:

For a time our lives may seem less harmonious and less satisfactory, and we may seem to have more trials and troubles than before. Since the shell of our former life and conceptions has burst asunder we find ourselves surrounded by new and bewildering conditions. At this stage the tender sprout of our unfolding spiritual consciousness may find it difficult to push up through the material conditions with which we seem to be hemmed in.

Increased Sensitiveness:

Our increased sensitiveness makes us suffer greatly from conditions, remarks, opinions and other vibrations which formerly affected us but little, and we cannot see how we can carry on while so surrounded and shut in, and hampered by such physical and mental conditions. This is the sprout stage during which we appear to be growing blindly, apparently blundering along through life, unable to see our way or the why and wherefore of events, and terribly irritated by little things.

Growing Pains:

Here is where a little knowledge of the Law and the process of spiritual growth will prove enormously helpful. For if we understand the Law we will realize that we are only suffering from the "growing pains" of a new life and an expanding consciousness. The tiny sprout can grow only as it absorbs out of the seemingly harsh environment of the soil which surrounds it just those particular chemical elements which it needs. First, these elements are transmuted from the seemingly inert soil into nourishing colloids by the living fire of the life-force focused upon them. Then they are built into living tissue which enables the sprout to grow. Just so must we learn to absorb the essences out of the experiences afforded by the soil of our environment and contacts, and build their lessons into the fiber of our character for our spiritual growth.

Recognizing Conditions:

We accomplish this not by denying outer conditions and experiences and refusing to have anything to do with them, or by refusing to recognize the changes they bring, but by *recognising them for what they are* and discriminating as to their meaning, significance and usefulness.

Live Life:

As we thus *learn to live life* and to face each condition and experience courageously, and with the positive force of the indwelling Christ-light flowing through us from within, that spiritual fire will fuse and transmute all the crude ore of outer conditions into the gold of spiritual growth. Then some day our consciousness will emerge from the darkness of ignorance and lack of realization, up above the hampering physical conditions and "conditioned reflexes," into a new world of spiritual light, realization and freedom. And this event will produce quite as great a change in our comprehension of what life on Earth is all about and why we come here, as the sprout experiences when it pushes up through the soil into the sunlight.

Growth in the Dark:

Then we will realize that all growth must start in the dark, and through pushing ever on and on through the darkness, thus gain the strength to stand the light without wilting when at last it emerges into the light. Then we will realize that as we absorbed the Waters of Divine Love from the Divine Mother, that have been poured out upon us, and which surround us, we have the whole assimilative and cohesive power of the Cosmos back of us to enable us to conquer and learn the lessons and assimilate the forces of our experiences and build them into growth that will enable us ultimately to reach up into the light of the Sun of Righteousness.

Drawn Upward:

Then we will realize that it was the light and warmth from the Sun of Righteousness that was drawing us upward all the time. Then we begin consciously to cooperate with the Law and put forth leaves and branches and make the growth that shall sustain the bud, which shall at last open into the flower of spiritual realization, with its golden heart in direct contact with the radiance of the Spiritual Sun.

Not Our Will:

In other words, we then realize that we came down from heaven not to do our own will: certainly not merely to give free rein to the gratification of the passions, appetites and desires of our human-animal instrument, nor even to be ruled by the petty vanities and ambitions of the human personality. We came to Earth to *unfold and manifest the pattern* and *express the qualities*, right here in material conditions, *of our inner Divine Self* which sent down its ray of spiritual life and consciousness for embodiment and an expression in this world of physical matter.

The Father's Will:

Jesus added another sentence of explanation to the one quoted above when He said: "And this is the Father's will which hath sent me, that of all which he hath given me I should lose nothing, but should raise it up again at the last day." At first glance this seems an extreme statement, impossible of fulfillment. For as we examine our selves and look at others in the world around us we seem to realize and express so little of all the divine powers which He hath given us as children of God, that the above statement seems so ridiculous as to be almost discouraging.

The Unawakened:

It may also seem to disprove the statement of Jesus when we see around us millions of people whose lives give no indication that they are here to do the will of the Father or have any conception of it, and who leave this world seemingly without having made any or but little advance. It therefore seems impossible that of all that he hath given them they should lose nothing. And so it would be impossible if we had only this one short visit to Earth that we call this life. For an explanation we must again fall back on the illustration of the Law as demonstrated in the acorn. If we keep this in mind we need not be discouraged; for of all the possibilities of becoming a giant oak it loses nothing, although its possibilities are only in embryo and latent until it starts to grow.

The Acorn Stage:

Just so is it with us. While we are in the acorn stage, when we are told of our divine inherent capabilities and possibilities they seem as impossible of manifestation as those of the oak must seem to the acorn. When we consider the traits of the animal body *which must be recognized* and *trained to be subservient* to the higher guidance of our reason and the well-known laws of life; when we consider all the selfishness, vanities and personal aggrandizement of the personality which must be trained to be subservient to the higher guidance of the Christ within—to say nothing about manifesting our higher spiritual faculties and powers—the task does indeed seem hopeless. But if we follow the same Law of Growth and assimilation which the acorn follows we are bound to attain corresponding results in the end.

The Law of Cycles:

For the acorn to grow and unfold into a mature oak it must follow the Law of Cycles which requires many summer-periods of growth and expression and many winter-periods of assimilation and consolidation, periods when the soft growth of the summer is consolidated into firm rings of solid wood. And the storms of winter only toughen its branches and sink its roots deeper into the soil.

New Growth:

But at each springtime the tree starts out with all the growth it has gained during the previous season with which to begin its new season or incarnation. Of all that has been given it of growth, unfoldment and attainment it should lose nothing, but should raise it up each spring as a basis of its further growth and unfoldment during the new life-season.

Many Incarnations:

Just so is it with us. For just as the oak cannot attain its full maturity in one season's growth, during one summer-period or incarnation, but requires many such seasons, so the Soul cannot unfold and express all that the Father hath given it in one season or incarnation. It takes us many summer-periods or incarnations of growth and unfoldment gradually to give expression to all the divine powers that are striving for manifestation from within.

New Lessons:

In each incarnation we learn new lessons, or if we have not learned the lessons of the past, we have to repeat past experiences or something like them, until their lessons are built into our consciousness and we are able to express more of the Real Self within, put out new twigs and branches, as it were, of our tree of life.

Storms Strengthen:

The storms of life through which we pass may indeed whip off some of our superfluous leaves, or certain superficial expressions of personality, and perhaps alter our mode of thought and life, but at the same time they toughen our branches and sink the roots of our consciousness deeper into the soil of truth and spiritual realization. Then during the winter-periods or the time between incarnations, we review the events of our past incarnations and learn the lessons from our experiences and consolidate them into definite Soul-growth.

Traits Built In:

Thus in the next incarnation we have all the traits that we have gained in the past built into our character and manifesting as innate tendencies with which to start out. They are the twigs of our last season's growth on which we put forth our new leaves of expression in this life. Thus do we progress from incarnation to incarnation, doing not our own will but the will of Him which hath sent us, until ultimately we learn to express all that the Father hath given us and lose nothing, but raise it up again at the last day, or during our final incarnation, when we have completed our cycle of manifestations in the flesh and are prepared to progress in other worlds.

Resurrection:

It is certainly not this imperfect and fallible human personality that is to be raised up at the last day. Still less is it this present incompletely evolved and incompletely perfected animal body, but the *perfected manifestation* of our Divine Self that is to be raised up at the last day. This is the true doctrine of the resurrection of the body. We repeat, it is not this *particular* body of flesh which we are using in *this* imperfect incarnation; for if all the bodies of flesh we have occupied during our many incarnations were to be resurrected, which one would we choose? Such an idea is, of course, ridiculous.

The Spiritual Body:

And yet there is a body that is "raised up at the last day." That is the *Light Body which we finally build up* by the purification, transmutation and spiritualization of certain atoms of our various bodies through "believing on the Son," as our text says, or following and manifesting the Christ within, until at our final incarnation we have built up a spiritualized vehicle or body through which we can manifest on any plane we wish.

Seeing the Son:

"And this is the will of Him that sent me, that everyone which seeth the Son and believeth on Him, may have life everlasting: and I will raise him up at the last day." The power by which the acorn unfolds is the power of the Sun, that focal point through which the light and life aspect of God is radiated to all forms of life in the physical world. But the acorn must "see the Sun" or come under its direct rays ere it can unfold into an oak. Yet it must do more than merely be in the sunlight: it must "believe on Him"—or must correlate with and absorb the forces of the Sun—before it can be "raised up at the last day" and complete its cycle of manifestation as the oak.

The Sun of Righteousness:

Thus must we follow the same Law. First we must "see the Son" or recognize the Ray of the Cosmic Christ-light within, as it manifests through our hearts. We must realize that it is the light from that Sun (Son) that is the source of our spiritual light and life, the power necessary for our spiritual growth.

The Cosmic Christ:

The Cosmic Christ is not only an infinite, celestial Power outside of, and as infinitely superior to, us as the Sun is to its ray embodied in the acorn, but is an individualized Ray of that Power manifesting within us, just as a ray of the Sun manifests through the acorn. For the Christ in us is a Ray of the Christ of God or the Cosmic Christ. To gain some realization of what this really means it would be well to repeat that sentence over and over again as a mantram or affirmation. "The Christ in me is a Ray of the Christ of God. The Christ in me is a Ray of the Christ of God. The Christ in me is a Ray of the Christ of God," etc.

Believe on Him:

But it is not enough for us merely to "see" mentally or recognize the Christ as the Son (Sun) of Righteousness. We must "believe on Him"; that is, *we must correlate with Him* through definite periods of meditation and recognition, or "seeing" Him and correlating with His force and building it into our lives as spiritual growth. Only so can we attain "life everlasting." We have come to realize that *our life here is only a temporary manifestation* for a few years in Earth conditions. Hence to attain "life everlasting" we must not only "see" Him but "believe on Him" to such an extent that we tune in to His force and thus are enabled to give expression to that immortal and Divine Self which we inherently are and *which must ultimately find expression* through the power of the Christ within.

Obscuring Veils:

He is hidden from our gaze, from our inner perception and realization, not because He hides Himself or wants us to stumble blindly along life's pathway, but because there are so many things in ourselves which hang like veils between us and Him, between our consciousness and His.

There are veils of misconception and misunderstanding; veils of materialistic thoughts, desires and emotions. Doubt is a thick dark cloud which hides reality from our sight. Selfishness and impurity are also clouds which veil Him from us.

Earth-born Clouds:

All such things send out their emanations like clouds which obscure our inner vision and blind us to the glory of Divinity. They are not we, *but they are ours* and we are responsible for them, hence we must spiritualize and redeem them. Our very desire for their purification and spiritualization casts them into the flame of the Christ-light, and the smoke that arises from their transmutation often envelops us. But just as the rising Sun dissipates the morning fogs, so will the Light of the Christ—the Sun of Righteousness—ultimately consume and dispel all the veils which hide Him from our sight. Then we shall see Him in His robes of glory, wreathed in tender smiles and radiant with Divine Love.

Those Who See Not:

Blessed are those who believe and love though they see not. Blessed are those who are being consumed, yet live; who are empty yet are filled,—filled with His love, His compassion, His understanding. Never allow the clouds of Earth conditions to dim your concept of His radiance or darken your lives. Doubt not, but believe; for belief opens the channel for the blessing. As we "believe on Him" so shall it be unto us.

Object of Existence:

The object of physical existence, therefore, is so to correlate with the Christ-force that we will quickly and easily, and without so much suffering from ignorance and mistakes, bring into visible manifestation the Divine Self within which we inherently are.

Practice Necessary:

To accomplish this we must resolutely turn all negative experiences into positive, constructive forces, and *consciously practice* expressing love, tolerance, harmony, happiness and co-operation. Thus will we reap the fruits of working in harmony with the Divine Law, instead of suffering from the results of acting and thinking contrary to God's laws.

Begin Now:

Begin now to measure all your thoughts and actions by some such standards as these: Are they (a) absolutely true? Could they stand the test of public scrutiny? Are they (b) absolutely clean? Are they expressions of true love and affection, a pure desire for Soul-oneness on all planes, or are they expressions of self indulgence or even animal lust? Are they (c) absolutely unselfish? Are they just and helpful to others as well as to yourself? Are they (d) absolutely kind and loving? If they can pass such tests as the above, *are they expressed* in such a kind and loving way that they will make others happy instead of hurting their feelings?

Instinctive Reactions:

And just as we react instinctively, before we stop to think, to the physical and mental habits which we have established, so should we formulate our ideals so definitely and positively that they become habitual, and we will react to them as instinctively as we formerly reacted to the lower habits and ideals.

Lords of Creation:

Thus will we gradually become the Lords of Creation— all that we have created—and shall make our bodies temples of the Living God. Thus shall we lose nothing of all that the Father hath given us but shall use it to help manifest heaven here on Earth. For we have learned that the *object of physical existence* is to *manifest the Divine through the human* by the power of the Christ-force flowing through us. Thus shall we accomplish our mission and fulfill our "Cycle of Necessity" or the reason why we come to Earth.

CHAPTER III

NEW DIMENSIONS

The crashing events of this Second World War have cracked through the crust of our former complacent acceptance of life and have made mankind aware of a wider field of understanding: a new dimension in life and consciousness.

Materialism Limits:

The truths taught and accepted by religion were held by science to be unproved because not physically demonstrable in scientific laboratories. But the crises of the present war have now demonstrated, in the laboratory of human experience, the reality of the principles taught by religion. For we now see that truth, honesty, ideals, love, compassion, brotherhood and co-operation are just as real as bombs, submarines and airplanes. And they have far greater power than the mightiest of war machines, for they govern the use of all the materials of the world.

Science has assumed that the physical world has only three dimensions which can be known and measured—length, breadth and thickness—until recently when a fourth dimension—time-space—has been added. For it is now admitted that time-space is not separate from other aspects of manifestation, but is the matrix in which all expression takes place.

Science has taught that there were only three dimensions to life, as expressed in the three primary biological urges or hungers, for food, comfort and sex satisfaction. But there is a fourth. Science has also taught that there were but three dimensions to mind—thought, feeling and will. But there is a fourth.

The Intellect:

These conclusions have been reached by one faculty of consciousness alone, the masculine polarity of intellect. Now the intellect is the instrument of thought-expression which formulates and translates ideation into concrete ideas. It is the sharp scalpel of the mind which dissects whatever it contacts. Of itself it is cold, analytical, separative and diversive. Its analysis of humanity has separated the oneness of mankind into races, nations, communities and individuals, each with majorities and minorities which establish pressure-groups for the attainment of their own selfish ends.

This intellectual analysis has been so material and separative that we have been taught that races and nations were almost separate species which could very well get along without one another. Yet it was found that intercourse was necessary and mutually advantageous. And as evolution advanced through savagery, barbarism and feudalism into modern civilization, certain agreements had to be entered into to regulate and stabilize such intercourse. And from these "gentlemen's agreements" a code of international conduct known as International Law was evolved. But with the recent resurgence of brutal barbarism all this has been ruthlessly trampled under the tread of mechanized brute force. Through this wanton aggression, in which all the rules of international conduct which centuries of respect for law had built up, and the freedom of many non-belligerent peoples, were swept away, a new consciousness has been born.

A New Consciousness:

The tragic mingling of many nations in common misery and suffering has broken down the artificial, intellectually-made barriers of race, language and boundary-lines, and has awakened a new fourth dimension in the consciousness of nations, namely, *the essential unity of mankind.* It has brought the realization that mankind is not made up of separate species, but is one: one community of human beings, all fashioned and projected into physical life by the same Creator. Hence they are all the children of the one God, no matter how diverse the names by which He is called.

It is true that philosophers and religious teachers throughout the ages have taught the essential oneness of mankind, but this was actually realized only by the advanced few. And it took the brutality of this war to break down the old intellectual concept of diversity into the realization that beneath the seeming superficial diversity there was an essential oneness of humanity.

This is but another evidence of our entry into the influence of the new Aquarian or Woman's Age. For it is only the cohesive feminine force of *love and compassion* that can reorganize the world. For love, not intellect, is cohesive, synthesizing, constructive and unitive. The intellect voraciously siezes everything it envisions and dissects it. On the other hand, Love flows out to enfold, integrate, develop, expand and perfect all it contacts.

Several Fourth Dimensions:

Just as a new fourth dimension has been found for matter, so has there recently been recognized a fourth biological urge or hunger. This is the hunger for *oneness through companionship*; the craving for oneness through harmonious and happy relations with our fellow men. It is this fourth dimension of *hunger for unity* that makes man a gregarious instead of a solitary animal.

And just as the satisfaction of this fourth dimension of biological hunger for companionship is recognized as necessary for the well-rounded life of the individual units of humanity, so it is being recognized as *an essential need* among the larger units of humanity, the nations and races. Thus it is futile and frustrative for any nation or race to strive to be sufficient unto itself. For as civilization advances and its interests broaden, it realizes that it is but one unit in a community of nations and races. And *it takes all these working together* to form our common humanity.

Another fourth dimension is one in the realm of mind. To the three dimensions of thought, feeling and will, there must now be recognized a fourth dimension, the selfless emotion of *compassion*. For the mind cannot be at peace with itself and able thus to experience true happiness while it contemplates the misery and suffering of the other individuals, nations and races which it contacts daily through travel and world-wide broadcasts.

To satisfy this compelling force of compassion, in our communities we organize hospitals, sanitoria, homes for the deaf and dumb, for the blind, the crippled and the aged. And to satisfy our compassion for other communities and nations we organize the Red Cross, "Bundles for Britain," "Aid to China," and means of feeding the children of the war-devastated countries.

Our Interdependence:

This new dimension of compassion makes us realize as never before that since humanity is one, what injures one community, nation or branch of the human family repercusses—either directly or indirectly—to the injury of all. Likewise, what benefits one redounds to the benefit and happiness of all. Until this oneness and interdependence is universally recognized and properly co-ordinated, we must expect social, economic and other disasters to continue to overwhelm us all.

The individual who is so occupied with the details of his personal affairs that he gives no thought and attention to the welfare of his community will be helplessly engulfed by the conditions of his environment in waves of graft, crime, bankruptcy and epidemics of disease, all due to some form of community pollution. The man who will not cooperate with his neighbors in the rule of his community must accept the conditions provided by those whose self-interest dominates.

Just so those nations which are so intent on their own affairs and on maintaining their own peace and neutrality that they do not accept their responsibility for world conditions, and so work for world peace and co-operation, will be engulfed in the conditions of world inharmonies which their isolation has permitted to develop, such as the onrushing tide of ruthless dictatorships. The nation which will not co-operate with other nations for harmonious world-conditions will be dominated by world tyrants.

To stop this useless self-destruction—due to failure to recognize the new dimensions of compassion and unity—and to prevent its subsequent resurgence after world peace has been restored, all humanity— or at least the leaders of nations—must grasp and act upon this fourth-dimensional cosmic concept of humanity's oneness, and therefore the intrinsic brotherhood of man.

As one noted sage has said: "It is only by close brotherly union of men's inner selves, or soul-solidarity, or the growth and development of that feeling which makes one suffer when one thinks of the suffering of others, that the reign of Justice and Equality for all can ever be inaugurated."

Demonstration Needed:

This realization must not remain a mere academic theory or metaphysical concept, but must be made *a working reality*. It must become *a law of life* which shall underlie not only political, but social, economic and all other relations between nations. For until the leaders of men have entered into this new dimension of world consciousness—the actual spiritual realization of the oneness of mankind—they will go on planning life on the same old narrow, selfish, nationalistic and self-frustrating lines. And thus they are bound to reap the same old tragic results.

Sacrifice Needed:

Psychology tells us that we must all make some sacrifices of our personal desires in order to live harmoniously and happily within our own consciousness for our own psychological salvation, that is, to avoid frustration and unhappiness. We must also make sacrifices to live harmoniously and happily with our neighbors for our own social and economic salvation and happiness.

The athlete denies himself many indulgences because his main purpose is to help his team to win the contest. Just so must nations sacrifice many national ambitions because their main desire is to live harmoniously and happily with other nations for their own national and international salvation, and for the welfare and happiness of humanity as a whole.

Personal Application:

To apply this new dimensional realization to our personal lives we must realize that the cosmic concept which enables us to enter this newly realized dimension of consciousness is the realization that our brief life here on earth is but one day's experience in the life of our Souls, our real Spiritual Selves.

For our consciousness is like a mighty hour-glass whose narrow waist alone touches the physical plane at one tiny point only. The lower cone of the hour-glass spreads out into the unfathomed depths of the subconscious realms, while the upper cone expands upward indefinitely into the sublime regions of the superconscious or spiritual realms.

The sand in an hour-glass can drop through its narrow waist only a few grains at a time as long as the outlet is unblocked. Just so can the grains of our superconscious or spiritual mind—our personalized ray of the Infinite Consciousness—filter through into our finite minds only a little, at a time, even when its outlet remains unblocked. For, naturally, the Infinite Consciousness can exhibit only tiny aspects of Itself to the perception of our little finite minds.

But if the outlet into our human consciousness is blocked because it is continually filled with personal, selfish and material thoughts and desires, the cosmic concepts from our fourth-dimensional consciousness cannot get through to expand our minds and hearts. And only by such expansion can we receive a flash of Cosmic Consciousness to guide us into harmonious co-operation with Cosmic Law and express it in acts of brotherhood and oneness.

The Cause of Suffering:

It is only by our failure to live in harmony with Cosmic Law that we bring upon ourselves the sorrow and suffering which inevitably result from our opposition to that Law. For the Law is like a mighty grindstone which should polish and perfect us and sharpen our wits to understand it. But if we resist its onward sweep it grinds us to dust. Our suffering is not the punishment of a hard-hearted God. It is simply the natural result of *our failure to co-operate* with the Cosmic Grindstone. But if we recognize and become one with it we ride upon it and are carried onward into unknown regions and upward into measureless heights in the cosmic manifestations of its mighty ongoing.

So it is not God who makes either wars or suffering, only our failure to respond to the Cosmic Law of harmony, brotherhood and co-operation. And we will continue to suffer from such conditions until we enter into and live out the new dimension of spiritual realization of the oneness of humanity.

Our prayers go unanswered unless we really correlate with Cosmic Law and allow It to flow through us into expression for the best good of all: unless to pious words we add potent acts which will materialize our inner realization. And that Cosmic Law includes the feminine pole of love and compassion as well as the masculine pole of life, intellect and will.

Leadership:

Under the Law of Love and Brotherhood it is the duty of the more advanced—those whose consciousness has expanded to grasp something of the cosmic concept of the new dimensions of matter, life and consciousness—to lead, guide and inspire the masses who are unable to realize the new dimensions into which the world-consciousness has entered. It therefore becomes the duty of you who can grasp this ideal to spread it abroad so dynamically that it will *crystallize into action* in your own life, in your family and community, and ultimately into the life of your own and other nations. For only as the qualities of these new dimensions begin their concrete manifestation in your personal life today *through action*, can they perfect your personal unfoldment and allow you to manifest more fully the Ray of God which you are within.

Feminine Forces:

Remember that it was the feminine forces of cohesion, synthesis, integration and growth that brought the whole universe into birth and manifestation. And through the gradual unfolding of its pre-determined pattern (evolution) it is those same feminine forces which are gradually bringing the Grand Plan to perfection.

Just so must the corresponding forces of understanding, tolerance, compassion, brotherhood and co-operation—manifested by both men and women—weld all nations into one harmonious humanity. Only thus can the New Age of love, brotherhood and co-operation be born and a perfected humanity be evolved which shall know not war.

Women's Duty:

Hence it is love and compassion—not intellect alone—which must be recognized as essential in the reconstruction of the New World Order. And as women are the focal points for the forces of the feminine polarity of the cosmos, it must be chiefly the enlightened women of the world—through their countless clubs, peace societies and other organizations—who must focus and manifest the Cosmic Love-force in the world today. Just as it was the women of France who carried the burdens and influenced the readjustment after the last World War, so must it be the women of the world today who must organize and *determine to have the decisive say* as to the conditions under which they and their families shall live in future generations under a World Federation of Humanity in which all nations participate.

Since it is easier for women to respond to the new dimensions of compassion and unity, it must be the women who, after the war is over, must mother the world, bind up its wounds and nurse it back to health, sanity, freedom and happiness.

What will you do toward this end—now?

CHAPTER IV

WITH COURAGE AND FAITH

The nightmare of the ages is upon us. The day of the karmic cleansing of the nations has begun. The changes necessary for the close of the old dispensation of separateness and individualism of nations and peoples, and the opening of the new dispensation of brotherhood and cooperation are at hand.

The Cosmic Plan:

It is the cosmic plan for the Aquarian Age that the barriers of boundaries, politics, language and trade which have kept peoples from harmonizing and fraternizing with one another—as they did even across the trenches during the holidays—shall be broken down and removed. But this adjustment should have come constructively through enlightenment and co-operation, instead of destructively through war. But since the natural forces of renovation and regeneration have been dominated by the forces of evil disguised as nationalism and race superiority, you must understand the process or your hearts may be filled with dark foreboding and even fears.

Since the last World War you have seen the fall of kingdoms, thrones and dynasties and the rise of many independent, self-governing nations. Now you are again witnessing the rise of the lust for power and world dominion, but this time the most ignoble means are being used. To the natural unrest and turmoil incident to changing conditions there has been added a boring from within, a penetration by alien plotters, treason by members of the "fifth column," and the "blitzkrieg" of sudden aggression against peaceful peoples. You have seen the pillaging and ravishing of democratic countries who asked only to be left alone to live their lives in peace. And now comes the new World War.

The Prophecies:

Both biblical and pyramid prophecies have warned that at the end of this dispensation, when "ye shall hear of wars and rumors of wars; see that ye be not troubled, for all these things must come to pass. . . . and upon the earth distress of nations, with perplexity. . . . men's hearts failing for fear. . . . And when these things begin to come to pass, then look up, and lift up your heads; for your redemption draweth nigh."

All sources of prophecy—biblical, pyramid, inspired— point out that this conflict was due to clean up the debris of the old cycle of materialism and selfish commercialism, to make way for the New Age of brotherhood and service. As we have already pointed out: "The time has now come when the accumulated mass of old Race-karma must be definitely met and conquered ere humanity can enter upon the new sub-race, its next step in evolution. . . . Europe is the first focal point because it was in Europe that the greater part of that Karma was engendered, *i.e.*, through the many bitter wars which drenched its soil in blood."[1]

Away back in 1917 we wrote: "The 'final battle' does not refer to the end of this present World War of nations, but to the close of the true Battle of Armageddon of which the present World War is but the *first phase*. . . . Just as changes must take place in the planet, so must they take place in humanity *through bloody wars*, strikes and other conflicts which will continue until all conflicts of man with man, and *man's resistance to the Divine*, are swallowed up, and out of the waters of affliction there shall arise a new and

---
[1] *The Philosophy of War*, Curtiss, 107, 103, 106-7.

greater humanity with true Brotherhood, Love, Peace, Harmony and Co-operation as its watchword."[1]

The Cosmic Concept:

Having heard remarks of discouragement from a devoted student which showed a lack of the *cosmic concept* of present-day conditions, we feel it our duty to make dear the laws back of the present crisis. To understand these terrible conditions, keep in mind several distinct points, namely, (1) that God established this world upon certain fundamental laws for the good of mankind, individually and collectively. (2) One of the most important of these laws is the Law of Action and Reaction or "Whatsoever a man soweth, that shall he also reap." Examined in the light of this law, nearly every colonial empire has at some time sown the seeds of selfishness, aggrandizement and aggression and the domination of weaker peoples. By force of arms they have invaded and seized other countries and peoples. Therefore do not be surprised to see those empires in their turn suffer invasion.

But (3) the great difference between their invasions and the present invasions in Europe is that their domination of the invaded countries was, on the whole, benevolent instead of ruthless pillage and regimentation and enslavement of the conquered peoples. Instead of *inaugurating* human slavery they have *abolished* it. Instead of religious persecution they did not interfere with the native religions, except to abolish human sacrifice—such as the burning of widows in India, head-hunting among cannibals, etc.—and allowed the natives to live their own lives while they were being assisted to higher standards of living. Therefore, while these great empires may suffer invasion and even lose some of their colonies, those countries that are now sowing the seeds of barbarism, cruelty and slavery must expect to reap similar results later on. Also the United States must some day expect to reap the results of its enslavement

---
[1] *The Philosophy of War*, Curtiss, 107, 103, 106-7.

of the Negro and its mistreatment of the Indians unless it makes up to both by such constructive treatment as will overbalance the destructive.

Karmic Reapings:

The next thing to keep in mind is (4) that these national karmic reapings are not a wilful punishment for our sins by a revengeful God. They are a natural and inevitable reaping of the causes each nation has set up. And until mankind learns that the fundamental laws of toleration, independence, freedom to pursue their own evolution, brotherhood and co-operation are the only basis for permanent peace and prosperity among nations, all will continue to suffer until they put these laws into effect through some sort of World Federation or Super-Government such as we outlined in our *Philosophy of War* and our essay on *The New World Order.*

That some such World Federation is possible was clearly seen by the poet Alfred, Lord Tennyson, in his pre-vision described in his famous poem, "Locksley Hall." Therein he tells us: "When I dipt into the future far as human eye could see; saw the Vision of the world, and all the wonders that would be; saw the heavens filled with commerce, argosies of magic sails. . . . heard the heavens filled with shoutings, and there rained a ghastly dew from the nations' airy navies grappling in the central blue. . . . Till the war-drum throbbed no longer, and the battle-flags were furl'd in the Parliament of Man; the *Federation of the World.*"

The next point to be remembered is (5) that this conflict is a manifestation of the battle between the spiritual forces which make for freedom, order and civilization and the anti-spiritual forces which make for regimentation, slavery and barbarism; between the forces of the Christ and the Anti-Christ. As we have explained in our *Spiritual War Bulletin* at the outbreak of the war: "Behind all the outer reasons, this is a war for the ultimate destruction of Christianity and the type of civilization which Christianity has built up. It is fundamentally a war between the forces of the Anti-Christ and those of the Christ; between the forces of darkness and the forces of Light; for only by the total destruction of all freedom of religious thought and ideals, and the complete domination of atheism, can dictator-despotisms be maintained."[2]

Importance of Faith:

The next idea to hold is (6) the great importance of keeping your faith in God, especially in the face of seeming disaster. As we said in our article on *Faith*: "The lesson for us today is that of true faith, that faith which is an attribute of the Soul, which is necessary to correlate the human consciousness with the Divine.... If we can have that *absolute faith* which comes from the realization of our oneness with the Divine, we can let the cosmic Divine Light flow through us and *our conditions* and allow it to solve our problems for us." The most tragic thing that can happen to your spiritual life is a loss of faith in God. Without faith only wretchedness and despair remain.

One student remarked that there could be no just God, nor even a beneficent overruling Providence, or He would not allow innocent and peaceful nations to be wantonly and brutally invaded. But of course he did not consider the Karma of those nations, as referred to above. God does not set aside His wise laws to answer our prayers for protection, even the prayers of a whole nation. Nor should you cry: "There is no just God," because His children break His laws of peace and brotherhood and have to reap the result.

Remember (7) that it is the duty and responsibility of each of you who are so privileged as to have the great truths of God's fundamental laws explained to you, to *take a positive stand* and to stabilize with words of cheer

---
[2] *The Philosophy of War*, Curtiss, 2.

and hope the faith of the unenlightened masses whose ignorance of God's laws leaves their minds a prey to chaos and fear. "Instead we must take courage and be supremely confident, for *Permanent Peace is the destiny of mankind* and cannot fail ultimately to materialize. Yet since man is God's vice-regent on Earth he can do much to hasten the day of the ultimate Permanent Peace, just as in ages past he has done so much to retard its manifestation."[3]

Another comforting thought to hold is (8) that each Soul chose to incarnate in the race and country, as well as in the family, in which he now finds himself. There he must be a positive factor by sharing in and helping to redeem, without complaining, the Karma of that nation which he helped to create in the past.

So-called Death:

Also remember (9) that the mere passing out of this earth-life through so-called death in war is not the most tragic thing in life, only a return home. It is merely laying aside prematurely your earthly garment and ascending into the next higher phase *of life*, as we all must do sooner or later. The really tragic thing in life and that which retards your spiritual growth and piles up tragic Karma for the future, is not death, but to perpetrate injustice, cruelty and human suffering. Therefore mourn not for the mere loss of life, the sudden ending of this incarnation. Instead, send out your love and compassion to all who are suffering from the cruelties of war. Pray that they may be given the power courageously to endure and that their suffering may be quickly ended.

Light Ahead:

And finally, remember (10) that *there is light ahead*. For there is nothing so dark that it cannot be lightened. There is nothing so poor that it is hopeless. There is nothing so bitter that it cannot be sweetened, nothing so

---
[3] *The Philosophy of War*, Curtiss, 73.

fearful that it canot be faced through the power of the Christ-within. Watch expectantly for the Light of Peace to break through. Do not allow your hearts to be dismayed or your minds to be dominated by newspaper and radio reports of the war. Before going to bed at night read something of a spiritual and inspiring nature. Repeat our *Prayer for World Peace** that your subconscious mind may have a constructive vision upon which to meditate during the night. "Watch for the beginning of the changes. . . . Be not dismayed at any trial or disaster, but recognize your great opportunity to spread the Light of Truth."

Keep away from places of inharmony, confusion and crowds, except crowds at religious gatherings, joyous musicals, cheerful plays and happy sports. When you have to mingle with the unenlightened, go forth charged positively with the radiance of the Christ-within, and spread cheer and comfort to all you contact. Walk as those who are sustained by the power of the living God, for verily He walks with you.

Sick of War:

Know well, dear students, that there is a Divine Wisdom that is greater than man's. There is a Divine Power greater than the armies of mortals. There is a Divine Love that is deeper than the love of power. There is a world that is sickening of disunion, of broken treaties and solemn promises, of antagonism, of war. And there is in the hearts of all peoples the germ of good which must and will awaken, and which will say: "We will have no more of this!" The very stars in their courses are fighting against the debauchers of humanity, and are gathering their forces for the inauguration of the New Day. Man *against* man instead of man *for* man can result only in destruction. The forward march of evil is bringing nearer the final judgment when His own shall be gathered together to establish His kingdom of righteousness on Earth.

---

* For this prayer see page 114.

Rest in Confidence:

"Rest in peace and blessing while subversive forces threaten you and cry out curses upon God and man. Pray for peace and plenty while famine stalks through the land. Pray for courage and stability while nations clash and continents disappear. For, lo, the time is at hand when all that has been foretold shall shortly come to pass. Be ye therefore prepared.... Let none of these things affright or move you. Recognize your oneness with the Divine, for lo, I am with you always, even unto the end of the world. Amen."[4]

VICTORY

Victory! Victory! children of Earth!
Something immortal in thee has had birth.
The gods of the storm-winds have taken their flight
And the angels of mercy are bringing thee Light.
    Anguish and sorrow no more shall depress.
The forces of heaven have brought thee success.

    Blessings immortal descend like the dew.
Look for thy blessing, it waiteth for you.
    Angels stand 'round thee and ever keep time.
Chant ye the victory in melodious rhyme.
    Children of Earth, fear nothing of harm.
The New Day is dawning. Look, look at its charm!

Victory! Victory! With happiness crowned!
Peace and sweet health shall fold thee around.
    Victory! Victory! To God give the praise.
Children of Earth thy Soul-senses raise.
    Thine is the power to work as to weep.
Out of thy life then all sorrows sweep.
  When tears and sorrow seem pressing thee down
Look up and sing Victory! this is my crown![5]

---
[4] *The Philosophy of War*, Curtiss, 153-4.
[5] Harriette Augusta Curtiss.

CHAPTER V

OLD CLOTHES

Effect of Clothes:

While in all but tropical countries clothes are worn primarily for protection and comfort, they have a far greater significance and influence. While it may not be entirely true that "clothes make the man," they nevertheless have an important psychological and even spiritual influence. They reveal not only taste, but individuality and character. A man cannot feel quite the same in overalls and sweater as he does in a new business suit, a Tuxedo or "tails." Nor can a woman feel the same in a kitchen apron or "slacks" as she does in a tea or ball gown.

Clothes Reveal:

Clothes are more than an index of taste and preference. They reveal much as to the stage of the Soul's unfoldment. Clothes that are worn to startle and attract attention to the personality are evidently expressions of vanity and self-aggrandizement, and reveal a young and undeveloped Soul. Over-youthful styles for the middle-aged call attention to the lack of youth and indicate a fear of old age.

How to Dress:

While we should all dress as becomingly and charmingly as is appropriate for the occasion, nevertheless middle-age should show a decided improvement in taste and refinement over the thoughtless impulsiveness and frank desire of youth for admiration. While all should dress and look as youthful, healthy and vital as their age and good taste permit, nevertheless maturity has a dignity, graciousness and charm which is not natural to youth.

Clothes Appeal:

Clothes should appeal to beauty, idealism and modesty, and contribute to true happiness. While "shorts" and "sun-tan" suits have their place in sports and bathing, they detract from our esteem and respect for the wearer if worn elsewhere. Flashy, pert styles tend to make flashy, pert girls, and are essentially vulgar.

Tasteful Dress:

Quiet, tasteful gowns may be beautiful also, and enhance the beauty of the wearer. They reflect the dignity and poise that come from an inner peace and spiritual unfoldment. They arouse thoughts of the ideal mother, home and family, while flashy clothes arouse thoughts of a night club hostess and all the frivolity, vanity and human weakness which she represents.

Psychological Effect:

According to the laws of emanation and radiation, clothes take on the psychological, magnetic and mental conditions of the wearer and the conditions under which they are worn. Because of their psychological effect, one can often dispel a discouraged feeling or a depressed mood by changing to a cheerful costume, one of bright and harmonious colors, especially one that has happy associations. On the other hand, clothes that strongly remind you of unhappy emotional conditions should be discarded as soon as possible, for they tend to revive those unhappy vibrations.

Cease Using:

Old clothes that have outlived their dignity or their more commonplace usefulness should not be kept and put away in the attic, the closet or the basement, but should be passed on to some needy person or welfare society where they can still give useful service to persons who are not sensitive to their vibrations. Especially you should not keep trunks or closets full of such old clothes and pour over them; for every time they are taken out and meditated upon they take your mind back to the time when they were worn and thus tune you in to those old conditions, ideas and emotions. Thus they tie you down to those old associations and make you re-live them. Those conditions are past and gone and you should have grown out of and beyond them and above them. So, why burden yourself with their unhappy and debilitating influences all over again?

Changing Clothes:

There is much to be gained by a change of clothes after a day's work. If you wear your office or working clothes at home you bring back much of the strain, worry and fatigue of the day's work. Hence it is difficult to take your mind off the day's worry and let it rest. It is also well to change—and even take a hot bath—after any especially disagreeable or inharmonious event or experience, that you may free yourself entirely from those vibrations and the more easily express the vibrations of peace, harmony and love of your own I Am Presence or Real Self, which is waiting to radiate from within.

Discard old Thoughts:

Old thoughts, ideas, habits and emotions are the old clothes of the mind. Once they are outgrown, why hark back to them? All that was good and constructive in them has been built into your character as new equipment with which you enter each new day or cycle of your life.

Therefore, deliberately discard and *refuse to re-live and react* to all the sorrows, fears, mistakes and regrets that have made your life hard, unhappy and unlovely in the past, and refuse to burden yourself with them.

No Mental Attic:

Have no mental attic filled with such ill-assorted and outgrown rubbish. Instead *carefully select* out of your lives, out of your hearts, out of the storehouse of your thoughts and feelings, beliefs and loves, only those that are constructive and conducive to your happiness and progress. For whatever you select you burden yourself with in your new cycle of on-going.

Prepare for New Experiences:

If you would be free to have new experiences, to have new ideas, learn new truths and take new steps upon the Path of Attainment, do just as you would if you were going on a long and important journey. Go into your inner closet, the closet of your mind and heart, and carefully view what you find, and choose only that which you should treasure. Do not try to dig up old and forgotten episodes from the dark corners of your memory. Look only for the bright and shining garments of joy and happiness, the bright jewels of faith, unselfishness and love. Decide which it is wise to carry with you and which it is wise to leave behind and forget entirely.

Select Your Vehicle:

If you were going on a long voyage your first care would be to select the ship most suited to your needs. Just so carefully should you select the spiritual ship or movement or teaching that is to carry you onward toward the mystical East where the Sun of Righteousness shall rise for you. It would naturally not be a new and flashy "speedboat" whose gaudy paint merely conceals its flimsy structure and whose claims for great speed to the Kingdom of God and the Christ-consciousness or shortcuts to Mastery and the Ascension serve only to disguise probable disaster. For the high seas of life are too tremendous for speed-boats.

Steady Growth:

Speed-boats are not needed on the spiritual voyage, for there is no time in eternity, and all eternity is before us. Also all solid attainment is a matter of *steady growth*, and, to change the figure, we do not want our spiritual growth to be of the hot-house type that fades when brought into the outer world or is destroyed by the first blast of a storm.

Results of Speed:

All those who try to rush through life take many false turnings which have to be retraced, often in sorrow and suffering. Even in the great ocean liners which rush through the seas at high speed, the vibrations of the engines and the shock of the waves are so great as to be most uncomfortable if not distressing and dangerous. What is needed is a modern ship, but one whose seagoing qualities and safety have been tried and tested through the years; one on which your friends have travelled for years and can recommend; one on whose structure (teachings) you can depend to carry you through the tides and storms of life; one whose captain knows, and can avoid the shallows, the tortuous channels and the dangerous reefs which wreck so many haphazard voyagers.

Friendships:

Once having selected your ship you should realize that your fellow passengers are to be close companions, with whom you will set up ship-acquaintances which may ripen into true and lasting friendships. And it is comforting to know that on this journey that is taking you to the distant realms of glory, your companions are selected Souls, brother and sister aspirants for divine realization.

They are in the ship of these teachings, not for any haphazard reason, but because, no matter what their outer personalities may be, each is here because he is seeking the same destination, the same great end. And he is here because he has paid the price. He has obtained his ticket by the travail of his Soul and has paid for it with the blood of his heart shed through his various life-experiences. And his ticket has been accepted and stamped by the hand of the Master of the ship. Therefore, all are worthy of your understanding fellowship.

Correlation:

Now if you were taking a ship for the Far East with a goodly company, and expected to spend weeks and probably months together in close intimacy and under all kinds of trying conditions, what would be the first requisites? Since you recognize that your own happiness on the voyage, as well as that of your companions, would depend largely upon your ability to correlate harmoniously and in a friendly and appreciative way with your fellow voyagers, the first thing you should make up your mind to do is to carry with you and radiate friendliness, cheerfulness, unselfishness and love. Since worldly wisdom suggests such a necessity for the success of your physical voyage, how much more important it is for the success of your spiritual voyage! And how is this to be accomplished?

Drop the Old:

Firstly, by leaving behind you the great bundle of old clothes belonging to your former life: the old inharmonies, fears, suspicions, resentments and selfishness that have been such a burden to you and which have held you back for so long. Or are you going to try to carry with you still the flashy garment of "pride of personality" which demands that you shall be recognized at your own estimation of yourself as someone of importance, instead of being willing to be judged by *that which you radiate* or manifest?

Don't Pity Yourself:

Are you going to be hurt and pity yourself and think all are against you if you are not recognized as you wish? Is that an expression of love? or of selfishness and vanity? Such self-importance and self-pity are some of the old garments that many an aspirant still clings to or hugs to himself. But it must be left behind, for it reacts even upon the body as kidney irritation and finally disease, just as resentment and anger react upon the liver, making one bilious.

Animal Emotions:

Until they are completely conquered, those demons of the animal-self, envy and jealousy, are ever present, causing misunderstandings, destroying friendships and often making even otherwise advanced students criticize and undermine one another. Beware, therefore, lest they subtlely poison your garments with their venom, and having spread their blighting influence, leave you in sorrow and remorse.

Examine Yourself:

Therefore, stop a moment and examine yourself. Can you and *do you* rejoice in the happiness you can bring to others? Can you and *do you* rejoice in the happiness your friends receive from other sources than yourself? Are you really glad when others do for your friends what you yourself cannot do? If you cannot quite honestly say yes to this self-examination, pray earnestly that the cleansing power of the Christ-love shall remove all these corroding stains of selfishness and vanity and wash your garments whiter than snow.

Self-Righteousness:

If you are not troubled with envy or jealousy, beware lest you wrap yourself around with that threadbare cloak of self-righteousness which makes you think that because you have not these particular failings, and that because you are on board this ship and are one of its company, you are therefore more advanced and hence more spiritual than your fellow travellers. Do you not know that that old garment is so threadbare that your companions can easily see through it how superficial and trifling your so-called advancement is? Do you think you can take these sources of inharmony and unhappiness with you without reaping the inevitable results?

Accepting You:

Perhaps you think such characteristics are the real you and the world must accept you as you are or you will have none of it. Do you think that the attention of the company will be so focused upon you that their quiet harmony will be disrupted and their peace upset, or that you can turn aside those earnest Souls who are so valiantly striving to progress and use all they have for the good of all? Indeed not. Such forces may cause inharmony and unhappiness, but it is you who will be broken, not the others.

Piques:

The piques, the slights, the hurts, the jealousies which you imagine another is sending you, you yourself are moulding into a weapon which will some day enter and wound your own heart. Only sorrow and suffering can come to you as long as you wear such a garment. Only when you throw it off and join your comrades hand in hand as they march along, singing the songs they catch from the angelic hosts, can you be one with them and partake of their happiness, and demonstrate the greatness of your Soul unfoldment.

The Great Soul:

The great Soul is one who has such a realization of the Divine Indweller, the Christ within, that he cannot be offended or hurt by lack of outer recognition or by slights to his personality. The great Soul is he who, like the Master Jesus, may be mocked, despitefully used, and even scourged, yet is so filled with the glory of the Christ spirit that he sees not the outer slights, feels them not, resents them not. He is charged so positively with the Christ power and is so busy radiating his cheer, comfort and helpfulness to others that he forgets to be selfish or inharmonious, and even that there is a personality to be offended.

Your Greatness:

You are all relatively great Souls in the process of greater or less manifestation through the garment of flesh, even if you have not manifested that greatness to any exceptional degree as yet. That greatness may still be too covered up with the old clothes of your earlier life, before you set out deliberately on this great voyage to the Promised Land. Therefore, look deep into the treasure chest of your life and heart and throw out the moth-eaten clothes of purely earthly desires, thoughts and habits, and take with you only those immortal, shining garments of love and compassion, of sympathy and unselfishness which are the livery of the Christ; for you cannot wear the old garments in the new life and be recognized as a follower of the Christ. They are not being worn by your companions on the voyage. Neither can you march side by side with your friends down the promenade of life for all to note and view while your clothes are covered with the grease spots of an unpurified personality.

Moth-eaten Garments:

Hence, if you find old moth-eaten garments of worldly ideas, of self-indulgence, self-seeking, self-pleasuring at the expense of principle and righteousness, gather up all such old clothes and expose them to the Sun of Righteousness that their hidden moths may be revealed and destroyed and you stand forth clad only in the pure white livery of the Christ. For if you had not such shining garments in your inner, spiritual wardrobe you would not be attracted to this great company or be on this voyage in the ship of this Cosmic teaching and have the comradeship of its followers.

Spiritual Garments:

Instead of clinging to the old clothes which are so bedraggled by the mire of earth, select the garments of the spirit, such as absolute truth, honesty, consideration of others, compassion and tenderness, and determine to bring them forth, don them and *wear them everywhere* in the light of day for the delight, help and encouragement of all. Perhaps you have not realized that you have been weaving such garments silently through the years.[1] Every heartlonging for the right, every aspiration, every effort to conquer a fault, every kind word, every unselfish deed has woven a strand into its fabric.

Your Garment:

No two garments are alike. No two are of exactly the same cut nor of the same shade or luster of shining, but since they are all woven of strands of harmony they all blend harmoniously; for they are all woven by the Spirit within seeking harmonious expression through the personality. Therefore, let the garment in which you appear before the world be an expression of the Real Self of you which dwells within, and not the ragged garment of the animal-self, patched with the faults and failings of the personality.

---

[1] See "The Curtain", in *Realms of the Living Dead*, Curtiss, 287.

Armor of God:

Or as the Bible tells us: "Wherefore take unto you the whole armor of God, that ye may be able to withstand in the evil day, and having done all, to stand. Stand, therefore, having your loins girt about with truth, and having the breastplate of righteousness; and your feet shod with the preparation of the gospel of peace; and above all, taking the shield of faith, wherewith ye shall be able to quench all the fiery darts of the wicked. And take the helmet of salvation, and the sword of the spirit, which is the word of God."[2]

Immortal Garments:

Thus shall you don the immortal garments of purity and truth, and stand before the world as a fearless and valiant soldier of the Christ. For the old clothes of the world have been put off forever and you are now clad in the livery of heaven.

---

[2] *Ephesians*, vi, 13-17.

CHAPTER VI

IDEALS

Ideals Rule:

Ideals rule the world for good or ill according to their origin and character. Their origin may be divine or human: either God-made or man-made. If high and pure and constructive, they express in peace, harmony, beauty and happiness. If low and impure and destructive, they express in inharmony, lack of symmetry, unhappiness and suffering.

Inner Pattern:

On every hand we see the inner moulding, directing and manifesting through the outer. In Nature the pattern of each genus, family and species of plant and animal, projected from the Divine Mind and manifested by the Hierarchies of Builders to express a certain ideal, determines the outer form and function. In fact, the planet itself, the solar system and all the galaxies of universes revealed by both the microscope and the telescope, are but more or less imperfect materializations of ideals in the mind of God.

Plan and Purpose:

From the vast and cosmic down to the finite and infinitesimal we see the plan, purpose and design of a superhuman consciousness which plans in infinite detail the grouping of the electrons in the atom according to the same law of co-ordination and harmony that groups the stars in universes. Everywhere we see forms evolving into more nearly perfect expressions of their ideals by discarding the less efficient and less useful forms to make way for ever more nearly perfect expressions of the ideals which bring them into manifestation, subject to the limitations of the density of the substances of which they are composed and the effect of the environment in which they are precipitated.

God-Consciousness:

This inner pattern or ideal which is back of all forms of manifestation is the vehicle of the outbreathing of the divine One-Life. And the forms which it animates are symbolic expressions of the God-Consciousness which underlies, enfolds and sustains all things, because it is the Soul or ideal of the universe. It is the eternal verities of this God-Consciousness which find expression in the fundamental ideals of spiritual truth whose expression is basically the same in all forms of religion and philosophy.

Thoughts Express:

In humanity our ideals mold our thoughts, and the thoughts that are repeatedly entertained or which strongly occupy our minds find expression in our words and acts, according to the first law of spiritual psychology. Every thought which we think positively will find expression through us *in terms of action*, unless counteracted by an opposite thought of greater power. Man, like other forms in Nature, has back of and within him his inner pattern or ideal, the divine Higher Self or the Ideal or Real Man. It is this Divine Self that is ever seeking unfoldment and expression through the limitations of the human personality, as the oak seeks expression through the acorn and the chicken through the egg.

Free Will:

But man has the God-given gift of free will. Hence, he can respond to and follow the *ideals* of his Divine Self or he can follow the *ideas* of his own human and limited creation. But unless his self-created ideas are in harmony with the eternal verities of spiritual truth in the spiritual or ideal world, they will clash with those higher ideals as they find expression in what are called the "laws of Nature."

Laws of Nature:

These so-called "laws of Nature" are but harmonious and constructive outpicturings of the fundamental Law of Manifestation, namely, from above downward, from within outward and from center to circumference. Therefore, *man never breaks a law of Nature*, for the Law is immutable. If man violates it and refuses to work in harmony with it, he reaps a destructive result. Instead of his breaking the Law, it is the unchangeable Law which breaks him, or he breaks himself against the Law.

Transition:

Those who really think for themselves and are not swept along on the tides of circumstance and popular fancy; those who give thoughtful and serious attention to the events which are transpiring around them, realize that they are passing through a period of rapid change of ideals in both their personal and national life; changes which affect all classes and conditions of people, as well as the Earth itself. For man cannot separate change and evolution from the Earth, since his body is of the earth, earthy, even though his Soul is divine.

Change Necessary:

Old ideas of government, old ideals as to political, economic, industrial, social and religious forms and relations are rapidly changing and new ideals and objectives are being established in their place. Now, change is essential to progress. That which is set in its form of expression gets into a rut, gets crystallized and cannot adapt itself to changing conditions. It really ceases to live dynamically and only vegetates until it decays. Hence, it is soon outgrown or passes away. Change, therefore, is necessary to readjust the outer to the expansion of the inner pulsating life of Nature, of man, of general conditions and of the planet itself, all of which are ever seeking new and higher forms of expression, as seen in the annual miracle of spring.

Divine Ideals:

But until man learns to found his new ideals upon the Divine Ideals of the Inner Man and the Inner Life, humanity will have to pass through a transitional period of chaotic conditions and consequent suffering while adjusting itself to the new man-made ideas until it finds out that glittering panaceas, presented by untutored and spiritually undeveloped minds, for the solving of surface problems—which are only the effects of inner and deep-lying causes—must fail. For *only ideals founded upon the eternal verities can endure*, bring about a constructive adjustment of conditions and harmonious and joyful results. How important then that these eternal verities be *repeatedly and insistently presented* to mankind in these days of confusion and man-made speculations, theories and makeshifts.

Mental Instruments:

Thought, intellect and reason are instruments of mighty power and importance, without which mankind cannot accomplish its mission in the world nor learn its lessons. But unless thought, intellect and reason are guided and checked and *controlled* by high *ideals*—instead of being determined by passing popular fancies, the desires of the flesh and the selfishness and aggrandizement of the personality—they are sure to be elevated to supreme importance, influence and control of the life, instead of being made subservient and willing and efficient instruments of the ideals of the higher consciousness—the Super-conscious Mind—of the Soul or Real Man, and subject to its Divine Guidance.

Guidance Needed:

We are all human beings indeed, but what kind of human beings we are depends upon the character of the ideals we hold and express. For this reason it is highly important that each student seek that Guidance in selecting the ideals upon which he is to base his life, thought and action, as found in the various avenues of teaching presented to him as Truth.

Ideas vs. Ideals:

Ideas may seem to rule in the intellectual world for a time, but unless they contain something more than mere intellectual force, something of the *ideal*, they sooner or later pass away. They may have been good *ideas*, but were not *ideals*. They must be vitalized by a spiritual force of a shorter "wave-length" and hence greater broadcasting power than that of mind. The idea of making the world "safe for democracy" and the subsequent setting up of several self-governing peoples was a good idea, and it swept Europe. The *idea* was grasped and accepted, but it was not made into an *ideal* by incorporating into it the basic principles of brotherhood and co-operation. Hence it was followed by an equally widespread wave of dictatorships. The idea of the freedom and political equality of women was long held by many, but only when it was vitalized by the spiritual ideals of Susan B. Anthony and her fellow pioneer workers did it become sufficiently radioactive to spread until it gained sufficient power to amend the Constitution of the United States.

Illumination:

For the earnest seeker of spiritual Truth, it is not enough then merely to have good ideas, important as those are. They must be illumined and expanded by an inner realization of the spiritual principles back of them so that they can expand from ideas into ideals. In fact, the greatest duty of the outer man is to know the ideal of the Inner Man and make it active in expression in his life.

Select Ideals:

We should have clearly thought out and firmly established ideals for all phases of our life. We should have ideals for the body, its perfection, health and happiness. This includes right ideas about food and proper food combinations, proper exercise, proper elimination of organic wastes, toxins and acids, etc. Since bodily states and conditions react upon the mind, and influence and color its mental states and reactions, it is important to establish ideals of perfection for the body and its functions. Always visualize the perfect ideal functioning of all its organs and parts.

Ideals of Mind:

We must also establish ideals for the mind. Realizing that nothing can affect us which we do not admit into our consciousness, we can set as our mental ideal the perfect mastery and control of our mind and all its thought-forces. We must remember that all thoughts that come into our consciousness are not created by us. Many of them are created by other persons. These combine with like thoughts of others to form great currents of thought— some high, pure and inspiring, some low, selfish, impure and lustful—which sweep over the minds of men either like gentle perfumed breezes from heaven or like cold, clammy fogs, vicious tornadoes of temptation, or stifling dust storms of self-indulgence which blind our eyes to the Truth and even shut out the radiance of the Sun of Righteousness.

Power of Thought:

Hence, we must carefully discriminate which type of thoughts we will admit into our consciousness and entertain there. For the second great law of spiritual psychology tells us that, "Every thought we accept and entertain we feed by our thought-currents and attention, and thus give it power over us." If it is not in harmony with the ideals of love, tolerance, purity, brotherhood and co-operation which we have set up as the standards of our own thought and action, then we must resolutely turn our backs upon it, shut our minds to it, and deliberately fill our minds with a realization of the Christ, the I Am presence, and let the radiance of its Christ-light so fill our consciousness that there is no room for lesser thoughts. Then its radio-active power will protect us from all impure, negative, critical and unworthy thoughts, and will neutralize and disintegrate them *without our having to concentrate upon* or fight them if perchance they have entered our minds. In other words, we must still the tumult of the rational mind and listen to the Still Small Voice of the higher, Superconscious or Spiritual Mind, and allow it to be the mighty, victorious, harmonizing and perfecting Intelligence which governs our world of consciousness and action.

Worship:

Most important of all, we must establish ideals of worship and devotion to God, the great and loving Source of all our life, consciousness and supply. For without worship, love and devotion, no amount of intellectual development can take us into the *spiritual* world, but only into the higher realms of the *mental* world. It is through the heart qualities and not those of the head that we contact the Divine. Once we understand this law and sincerely desire to draw closer to the loving Christ and let Him fill our lives with joy and blessings and guidance, we must open our hearts to Him in prayer, worship and ardent devotion.

Meditation:

For this purpose we must have definite periods of meditation when we relax all tension of body and of mind, put aside all thoughts of the outer world that may have occupied our minds, and still all its activities while we listen to the guidance of the Still Small Voice in our hearts, which will reveal the ideals for which we should strive. For if we ask sincerely and devotedly for that guidance we will be given the inner conviction and assurance of that which is best for us.

When Ready:

If it is enlightenment and instruction that is needed, in some and often remarkable way we will be brought into touch with that avenue of teaching which is best adapted to our stage of unfoldment. Those who find in the Truth expounded by these Teachings the most spiritual and inspiring ideals, as well as the most comforting, satisfying and practical solutions of life's problems, should give them such serious study that they become a part of their mental and spiritual life, a firm foundation of ideals upon which they can stand secure and firm. Then they cannot be turned aside by the popular, but often misleading, fads of the day. Thus will this Teaching develop a united body of advanced thinkers and devoted disciples all seeking to demonstrate and spread the same high ideals to all they contact. Thus they will become a bulwark or safety-station for humanity in the midst of astral mirages and temptations, in the revolutionary conditions of the outer life through which humanity is passing, and among the swirling and conflicting currents of mere human opinion as to what is Truth, what is cosmic philosophy, what is true spiritual teaching, and what is ideal.

Christ Ideal:

Let us therefore determine first to define our ideals of life, of conduct, of thought, word and deed and then to make them so real, so definite and concrete *by repeatedly concentrating upon them* that we will react to them instinctively before we have time to think. For there is no standard short of the Christ-ideal that is worthy of our attention and attainment.

Our Ideals:

Just what is our ideal of life? Is it the uncertain accumulation of this world's goods whose loss leaves us barren and desolate, and which we have to leave behind us when we leave this world, or is it the accumulation of spiritual treasures which we do take with us? Is it the attainment of fleeting power and position in this world of temporary sojourn, or is it the attainment of powers which determine our position for all time in our real home or heavenly world? Does it include a perfect body, an illumined mind and a lofty Soul only to satisfy the pride of personality, or to attain the Christ-ideal which will be expressed so radiantly as to inspire others to strive to attain and manifest that ideal?

CHAPTER VII

THE WOMAN'S AGE

Cyclic Law:

Cyclic Law rules manifestation; for all manifestation takes place in cycles of outbreathing and inbreathing. Day follows night. Summer follows winter. Nations have their birth, reach their zenith, decline and pass away. Subraces and Races arise, flourish and are no more. Likewise Age follows Age. "The thing that hath been, is that which shall be; and that which is done is that which shall be done; and there is no new thing under the sun."[1] And yet each new cycle is not a repetition of the previous cycle; for manifestation is not in a circle, but in a spiral. Each renewal of expression is on a slightly higher level, for each season's growth builds on the branches grown last season. Therefore, existence is not a hopeless round of repetition, for each cycle is a new opportunity for greater expression.

An Age:

While the Sun finds its cycle of expression during the year in the twelve signs of the zodiac, there is a still greater cycle called the *Magnum Annus* or Solar Year. This requires approximately 26,000 years to bring the heavenly constellations back into their same relative positions.[2] And this Solar Year is also divided into twelve signs. Each of these twelve periods is approximately 2160 years in length, and each is called an Age. Each Age

---
[1] *St. Matthew*, xxiv, 30.
[2] For details gee *Message of Aquaria*, 23, and *Key of Destiny*, 36, Curtiss.

takes its name from the sign which is ruling at the time. Thus, we are just closing the cycle of the Piscean and are entering into the Aquarian or Woman's Age. So every 2000 odd years our solar system enters into a new region in space, into a definite new division of the greater zodiac. This concentrates upon the earth certain new forces and new combinations of old forces which naturally affect everything upon it. For instance, astronomers tell us that the gigantic storms in the photosphere of the faraway Sun—visible as the so-called "Sun-spots"—have a marked effect upon the weather, also upon the magnetic currents of the earth, so much so that they interfere with radio reception. And just as cosmic forces affect earth vegetation, so do the forces of the New Age affect all humanity.

The Aquarian Age:

Astronomers are still at variance as to whether our planet Earth has actually entered into the Sign Aquarius in the celestial zodiac. But all students of mystical science, and most astrologers, agree that we have at least entered into the influence of its penumbra or aura. Many consider that we entered the Aquarian Age with the entry of Uranus into Aquarius on February 12th, 1912.[3] Since that date humanity has been subjected to the outpouring of these new streams of cosmic force, especially the love-stream of the Divine Mother, and has been reacting to it in various ways. Since humanity as a whole requires considerable time to react to new cosmic forces, at first only the more sensitive and advanced can respond. And even they seldom understand the reason for the new ideas and the great urge to bring them forth which surges within them. But nevertheless they become the pioneers and leaders in all the advanced lines of thought and action of the day. But regardless of the exact date—which mat-

---

[3] When the Sun also entered Aquarius by precession.

ters little in so long a cycle as 2160 years—we know that the Clock of the Heavens has struck the hour and a New Day has dawned for mankind, and especially for the rapid unfoldment of women.

The Woman's Age:

Aquarius is called the Woman's Age because the forces emanating from the constellations in Aquarius are essentially feminine in their influence. A symbol of a man pouring out water upon the ground also indicates this influence. For as water is the essential, nourishing principle without which no life can be brought forth, it is an expression of the Divine Mother-love of the Godhead, and therefore properly symbolizes woman, who is the human embodiment of that force. In fact, even the name of the feminine or love-aspect of the Godhead in nearly all religions is connected with water, such as the latin *Mare*, the sea or the Great Deep, and in the Christian religion as *Mary*.*

Man's Domination:

Aquarius is the 11th sign, the 11 symbolizing a new beginning, an Age when the feminine force of the Divine Mother is being poured out in abundance that the womanhood of the race may have greater opportunity for unfoldment. In past ages it has been man's force and man's ideas that have dominated not only business, but society and even religion, wherein the masculine aspect or the fatherhood of God has been emphasized rather than the motherhood. During the reign of the masculine qualities woman has been regarded as a possession of man, and when not a chattel owned for his pleasure she was at least a plaything for his delight and comfort, or perhaps even an idol to be worshipped. But man was always in possession and control. Now man's period of rule and domination is about over. He has proved by his failure to

---

* For details see *The Key of Destiny*, Curtiss, 144-5.

bring peace, harmony and happiness to mankind, through force without love, that it is not good for him to rule alone.

The Allegory:

In the allegory of the Garden of Eden man is represented as being alone at first, but containing both the masculine and feminine attributes within the one androgynous body. But as that early ethereal body became more materialized and came under the law of the physical plane—the Law of Duality—the androgynous form could no longer contain the expanding feminine principle and the sexes had to separate. This physiological event in the evolution of the body is symbolized by Eve's being taken from Adam's side as a rib. We know it was not a literal rib, for man has as many ribs as woman. None are missing. Why, then, should so curious a symbol as a rib have been used? Because it perfectly illustrates what took place.†

Feminine Qualities:

The down-pouring of the Aquarian force is quickening the feminine qualities in both men and women, and women are coming out of their seclusion in the home and taking their stand side by side with man in the governing of the affairs of the world. Woman can no longer be regarded as a mere "rib"[4] or part of man, an appendage or a "side issue." For even a rib is not an appendage or afterthought, but is an essential part of the structure of the body, without which the vital organs could not be maintained in their normal positions or receive their needful protection. Just so woman is an integral and vital part of the body of humanity and the structure of society. She can no longer be hidden in the body politic, but must step out and come forth, as the rib was taken out of Adam. She must manifest her true self and take her true place as

---

† For details see *The Truth About Evolution and the Bible*, Curtiss, 87-90.
[4] See *The Truth about Evolution and the Bible*, Curtiss, 87-90.

a vital and ruling factor, not only in the home, but in the world's affairs, and in the life of humanity.

Crusades:

But how is she to overcome the customs of ages and make her influence felt in a world so dominated by man? At first it seemed hopeless, but by responding to the urge of the down-pouring of the Mother-force, she has organized various great crusades for political freedom, temperance, educational reform and other progressive and uplifting movements. As you know, her efforts have already won her political freedom in England and the United States and elsewhere, and has even amended the Constitution of the United States in her favor. And in France the changes made in the Civil Code have released the French women from obedience to their husbands, given them the right to have bank accounts in their own names, sue for damages, inherit property, etc.

The Goal:

But the winning of political freedom is not her ultimate goal. It is only one step toward a destined end. For the goal of woman is not to be a politician or an office-holder, although society needs her influence in both those fields. Her mission is to embody and express the Divine Mother qualities for the uplift of the whole human family.

Changing Conditions:

The emergency of the world war forced millions of women out of the round of domestic life into the larger life of service to their country and its soldiers. Changing economic conditions since then have forced other millions from the home into the office or factory. And woman has proved her ability to succeed in all these new tasks. In countless cases the manifold responsibilities of the cottage or country home have been replaced by the simpler duties of the flat or apartment. How should woman make use of her new found time and freedom? For one thing we would suggest that all who realize the good they can accomplish for their community and their country, as well as for themselves and their families, by their united efforts in constructive endeavors, should carefully select some such activity— club, church, society, etc.—in which they can take a sincere and active interest for the culture or uplift of mankind.

Woman's Influence:

Women are already having a vast, constructive influence in their clubs for cultural and artistic ends, in Peace Societies, Parent-Teachers Clubs, and their support of all manner of metaphysical, mental science, mystical and religious movements. So their ideals of culture, education, health, child welfare and social service are gradually uplifting the peoples of all lands where they are actively cooperating, in spite of the seeming laxity of the noisy and therefore conspicuous minority of aimless pleasure seekers. Our suggestion applies with especial force to those who are not blessed with families and who therefore have more time for outside activities and recreations. But care should be taken not to engage in too many such activities or one is apt to dissipate one's forces too widely and so accomplish less good.

Excesses:

No doubt in her new-found freedom woman has gone and may still go to extremes in some ways, but time and experience will solve that problem. At first many felt that they could best demonstrate their freedom from man's domination by aping man's ways. In an unthinking spirit of bravado many thought that it was "smart" and "modern" to imitate his bad habits, such as cocktail drinking, gambling and smoking. Such habits are far more deleterious to woman than to man because of her more sensitive nervous system. They also tend distinctly to coarsen her mental, moral and social fiber, as well as impair her normal fertility. They also open her more easily to invasion of both her body and her mind by low astral forces which commonly swarm around barrooms and similar places. The woman of the New Age must regard her freedom as something more than freedom to ape men. On the contrary, it should make her more able to raise the standards of life and action of both herself and her family. For the more inharmony she raises, the fewer advanced Souls will incarnate through her to be raised by her.

Woman's Place:

Man's age-long refusal to give woman her true place beside him in the world's affairs, as well as in the home, has perverted her talents and forced her to use the power of her feminine charms to entice and enslave man so as to gratify her vanity, her ambition, her comfort and her economic security. But now her victory must be one of moral and spiritual leadership. The woman of the New Age must use her new freedom not to *lure* man but to *lead* him. She should no longer play upon his chivalry merely to lead him to the altar of matrimony, but to the altar of worship; not to social and economic heights, but to spiritual heights. She should seek to stimulate not his passions, but his possibilities, his aspirations and ideals. For man can easily be inspired and led to support almost any altruistic crusade by ideals sincerely expressed and actually lived, where he could not be cajoled, forced or driven. And since recently published statistics (1938) show that there are 1,645,000 more women than men in Great Britain, their influence, when properly directed, should be overwhelming.

Preparing Food:

Woman should still prepare the food for man, spiritual as well as physical. She should see to it that it contains plenty of live foods, full of vitamins—spiritual as well as physical—and properly combined to produce spiritual health and vitality as well as physical.[5] For just as the physical food she prepares contains her personal magnetism and the vibrations of her mother-love and her degree of happiness while preparing an appetizing meal, so should the spiritual ideals she presents be bathed in the vibrations of her intuition and her spiritual love for the unfoldment of the Divine in her family. Many a meal, although composed of proper ingredients, is made unsatisfying and even irritating by the thoughts of hurry, irritation and resentment if the one who prepares it is in an unhappy mood. If she establishes the habit of singing or humming as she cooks she can revolutionize her meals, and the family life as well.

The Bread-maker:

Woman should therefore be the symbolic if not the actual bread maker, and may even help with the bread winning upon occasion. But she should also see that her family is supplied with those spiritual truths and ideals which are the Bread of Life,[6] baked in the fires of Divine Love. The modern man and his inquiring-minded children can no longer be fed on the dry crusts of out-of-date theological dogmas; for without the feminine waters of love any food dries up and is tasteless and unsatisfying. Neither will the modern mind be satisfied with the coarse fare of literalized and materialized biblical interpretations and ritual, of predestination, hell-fire and infant damnation, that satisfied his less analytical forefathers.

Old Time Religion:

"The old-time religion is good enough for me" is the slogan of an unthinking mind and an unprogressive spirit which should have no place in the New Age. It applies

---

[5] See *Four Fold Health*, Curtiss, and also *Vitamins*, Curtiss.
[6] See lesson on *The Eucharist, The Bread*, Curtiss.

only to those who are willing to put up with the old time ox-cart methods of transportation and the tallow-dip methods of illumination. Woman should make the spiritual bed for her family as well as the physical, for only so can they attain the spiritual relaxation, rest and refreshment needed for their happiness and Soul growth.

Motherhood:

Just as the woman of the New Age is neither merely a politician nor a factory worker, so is she no longer merely a child-bearer and household drudge. The woman who really belongs to the New Age can no longer be merely a housekeeper or even an idol to be worshipped. Since it is her mission to represent and embody the qualities of the Divine Mother[7] on earth, to her belongs the moral and spiritual leadership of mankind, for necessarily she must be the mother of the New Age. And she can also be the mother of a New Race if she will recognize her opportunities and make the mental and spiritual conditions necessary to attract advanced Souls to her from the higher realms. It is now more than ever her great opportunity to influence the future of the Race by deliberately attracting to her and giving incarnation to those Great Souls who will become the leaders in the various affairs of the New Age. For she attracts variously developed Souls *according to the ideals she holds*. Many of the Great Ones have been waiting for ages for the right era and the right mothers who can give the right conditions of peace, harmony, thought, idealism and spirituality in which they can incarnate and accomplish their mission. For the New Race cannot incarnate in conditions where material ideas of wealth, power and selfishness predominate. And even those now in incarnation are limited in their expression by the prevailing race thought.

---

[7] See *The Divine Mother*, Curtiss.

The Childless:

And even if a vast number of women have not the opportunity to bring forth bodies in which the many Souls now awaiting incarnation can come to earth—although that is one of the most exalted services women can render the race—they should be giving embodiment to the many new spiritual ideals of beauty, harmony, justice, love and righteousness which are also awaiting an opportunity to incarnate for the inspiration and guidance of mankind during this Woman's Age. Hers being the intuitive type of mind which can grasp the essence of Truth without the laborious process of logical reasoning, she is the one to grasp and bring forth the new ideals for man to embody and establish in the outer world.

The Bringer-forth:

The wave of feminism now sweeping the world is the result of the Divine Mother-force now being poured out upon humanity from the sign Aquarius. It is therefore stimulating the feminine aspect of all mankind with a great desire to bring forth new conceptions of life and human society, new realizations of truth and new conditions for the health, happiness and uplift of mankind. And because of her mission as the Bringer-Forth, woman must be the leader in all social activities. The fate of nations, the Race and even the Planet depend upon woman's recognizing the great opportunity which the Woman's Age can give her to accomplish her true and greatest mission in humanity.

Youth:

The saying that "the hand that rocks the cradle rules the world" is still true, but is woman still rocking the cradle? Are not many rather "rocking the boat" of society by their neglect of the cradle for card and cocktail parties and other frivolities? The so-called "laxity of youth" now so widely deplored can be traced directly to the laxity of their home training in ideals, because their cradle was not properly rocked. Woman's great opportunity to influence the growing mind must be inspired by high ideals and organized to attain definite ends, such as truthfulness, courtesy, respect for ideals and spiritual principles, worship, etc. Woman's true place is that of Priestess of the Home and Family, whether that family be her own private family or the wider family of her school, her business associates, her church, her clubs or her social group. There *she is responsible* for the ideals and standards set for the spiritual life of the home or group.

Woman's Responsibility:

Therefore upon woman rests the moral and spiritual leadership of the Race, as upon man rests the responsibility putting her inspired ideals, as well as his own, into executive action and manifestation. Neither is superior to the other, any more than one hand is superior to the other. Nor can one usurp the proper functions and duties of the other. Both must work together like the right hand and the left to accomplish the tasks common to the welfare of both. Man and woman must go forward hand in hand in harmony, love and mutual self-respect if the New Age is to be ushered in in peace and prosperity and its ideals attained.

Woman must keep ever in mind her true role as the inspirer of mankind. When she cannot attain her ideals through feminine means she should plan to have them manifested by man rather than trying to use masculine means herself. Thus will woman take her place as the one who can lift the Veil of Isis—the Divine Mother—and initiate her help-meet into the realization that the steady radiance of Divine Love should shine out through all human contacts and relationships.

The Golden Apple:

If woman can be said to have given man the green Apple of Discord which brought about the so-called "fall of man"[8] and to have introduced evil into the world, so must she now give man the golden Apples of Hesperidies, which through her spiritual illumination she has plucked from the Tree of Life to uplift man, and so redeem any mistakes she may have made. It is therefore now time for her to sink all petty differences of outlook and method, and unite in the one object of bringing forth the ideal in the daily life, that woman and the Woman's Age may the sooner accomplish their manifest destiny.

---

[8] For details see *The Truth about Evolution and the Bible*, Curtiss, 60 and 221.

CHAPTER VIII

SMILE, SMILE, SMILE

A Beaming Smile:

A smile is like a sunbeam. It lightens up everything it touches. It sheds a mellow radiance on social intercourse that no blaze of intellect can equal. A happily smiling person upon entering a room can dispel the gloom, overcome the cold, formal reserve of the gathering, put people at ease and often set them chatting gaily with one another. *Just try it.*

Costs Nothing:

A smile costs nothing, but creates much. It is the easiest thing to give, and it brings great returns. It enriches those who receive it without depleting those who give it. None are so rich that they can get along without it. None are so poor but are made richer by its radiance. *Just try it.*

Twinkling Eyes:

A sincere smile is always appreciated. It keeps one from being tense and rigid. It "breaks the ice." Few have the courage or the inclination to try to thaw an iceberg, but a warm smile will do it. *Just try it.*

Smile in a Jam:

Smiling in a traffic jam prevents you from fretting or chafing at the inevitable. It restores a sense of values. It relieves many a tense and difficult situation. *Just try it.*

Smiling Fortifies:

Smiling helps you to live with people, not just among them. If you smile you cannot be embarrassed, hurt or angry over remarks or even insults. And if you lose your temper you lose your power of reason and judgment. *Don't permit it.* Just smile and note the results. *Just try it.*

Sense of Humour:

Watch for the amusing side of things. Learn to laugh at yourself. A situation is just as funny when it happens to you. Laugh with others, not at them. Kindliness and good-will win hearts. Give a kindly smile. *Just try it.*

Springs of Cheer:

A true smile comes not from the intellect but from the heart. And it warms the hearts of others. Cheerfully smiling people are like bubbling springs which refresh, stimulate and enthuse. *Just try it.*

Smiling Scrap Book:

Clip anecdotes, and other items of a cheerful nature, and make a book of them to cheer and refresh yourself and your friends. *Just try it.*

Sympathy:

A smile of sympathy can cheer the bereaved and lighten their sorrow. *Just try it.* A loving smile can win the heart of a child when even candy is refused. *Just try it.* A friendly smile can put over a business deal which no amount of cold intellectual argument could close. *Just try it.* A smile is more endearing than a brilliant intellect. *Just try it.*

Companionship:

A smiling person, even if uneducated, is a more pleasing companion than a highly educated person who is coldly intellectual. *Just note it.*

The Memory Lasts:

A smile happens in a flash, but the memory of it sometimes lasts forever. It creates happiness in the home, brings success in business, fosters fellowship in the lodge, and is a valued courtesy that should be given without stint. *Just try it.*

Cannot be Bought:

A smile cannot be bought, begged, borrowed or stolen. It is no earthly good until it is given away. It is sunshine to the sad and Nature's best antidote for trouble. *Just try it.*

Types of Smiles:

There are several types of so-called smiles, but only that smile which is inspired from the heart is the true smile. An insincere smile is not a true smile, only a smirk. An enigmatic smile, like that of Mona Lisa, although it may be intriguing, is not helpful. It makes people uncomfortable because it is not frank and honest, and may be suspected of being critical, derisive or contemptuous. A wry smile is but a grimace. A smile of mere animal pleasure or satisfaction is only a grin. A sinister smile is but an evil leer. With such a smile, as Shakespeare says: "One may smile and smile and be a villain still."[1] But all such are but perversions of a true smile.

Importance of Smiling:

At first sight smiling may not seem to be much of a spiritual expression, but in reality it *releases the power of the I Am* into outward manifestation. The importance of smiling is therefore many-fold. First in its effect upon ourselves. It makes us responsive to the expression of the inner harmony and love of our Spiritual Self. That expression through us is developed by the frequency and

---

[1] *Hamlet*, Act I, 5.

the degree to which we react and express that inner love and harmony.

Relaxes Tension:

Smiling relaxes all tension of both mind and body, and releases various mental repressions and complexes which, if long continued, are apt to find destructive expression. It helps to neutralize and dissipate depressing thoughts and emotions. If one who is crying can suddenly be made to smile, how the emotional state is changed and how quickly the tears disappear! *Just try it.*

Ill-humour Evaporates:

How quickly ill-humour also evaporates before a good-humoured smile. Recently a taxicab ran into our car and the frowning driver seemed ready to curse us, but when we smiled good-naturedly, his frown relaxed and he waved us a cheerful "O.K." We also *practice smiling on all who serve us*, postman, milkman, gasoline attendants, store clerks, etc., and do not stop until we get a smile in return, no matter how forbidding their mien at first. *Just try it.* But to secure such constructive results the smile must be sincere or it cannot convey the positive radiations which will overcome and supplant the negative vibrations.

"Smiles the cushions are that soften
Man's hard knocks that come full often.
Thru the wrinkles he seems to see
A goodly world, with which to agree."[2]

Laughter:

Smiling naturally leads to laughter, which is even more relaxing and releasing, as the outer expression of an inner joy. Such relaxation has a stimulating and constructive

---

[2] *Smiles and Reflections*, Clark, 30.

effect upon all the bodily functions. In fact, laughter is a physiological necessity for health. Not only does the brain and nervous system require it for relaxation, but the heart-beat is accelerated, the blood is oxygenated and kept red, and the quickened circulation flushes the cheeks with a rosy hue. It also promotes digestion and stimulates the functions of all the endocrine glands and other internal organs. Therefore, for health's sake alone *we should make smiles and laughter so habitual* that they will bubble up *spontaneously and sparkingly*, like water from a spring. *Just try it.*

Smiling at Dinner:

These psychological and physiological effects are so well known that they are taken advantage of by the hostess who is planning a dinner party. She is very careful to invite only those who are known to be harmonious and happy with one another; and smiles, jokes, wit and laughter are encouraged, while controversial subjects which might lead to arguments and inharmony are banned. For without harmony and laughter the dinner is a bore, and even the most delicious viands are less enjoyed and may lie undigested because of tension or mental inharmony. Shakespeare says: "Loose now and then a scattered smile, and that I'll live upon."[3]

Why Smile:

Frankly, would you not like yourself better if you smiled more? *Just try it.* Why is this? What is there about a smile that elicits such favorable reactions from others? What is the law back of it? And how can we apply that law so that we may make it work for us? It is the result of the Law of Radiation from the I Am in action. Let us see why.

---

[3] *As you like it*, iii, 5, 103.

Law of Radiation:

Every living thing in Nature is but the vehicle of a center of force, life and consciousness in the invisible world which is seeking manifestation in the physical world. Therefore, every living thing is a battery which is charged with its invisible, dynamic forces. And since all forces radiate their vibrations, even if they do not emit actual emanations of themselves, they are centers of dynamic radiations.

Skotographs:

It is said that even a leaf of a growing plant is so charged with its radiant life-force that it will take a *skotograph* or shadow-picture of itself if placed upon a photographic plate. Following the same Law of Radiation, we also are batteries of radiating forces—odors, physical magnetism, mental, emotional, psychic and spiritual forces—which impinge upon and *produce some form of reaction* from everything and every person they contact, whether recognized and immediately expressed or not.

Ebb and Flow:

According to the Law of Ebb and Flow which rules all manifested life— even our incarnations—everything that is emanated or put forth from any center of radiation or manifestation must ultimately return to its source, bringing with it the net results of its manifestation. According to this law our Real or Spiritual Self returns to Its divine Source bearing with It the net results of Its incarnations on Earth.

Vibrations Return:

According to this same law every word we speak, whose vibrations we put upon the air, will bring back to us its fruition sooner or later. Jesus recognized this law when

He said: "Every idle word that men shall speak, they shall give an account thereof in the day of judgment"[4]

> "The world is like a mirror,
> Reflecting what you do.
> And if you face it smiling,
> It smiles right back at you!"

Our Emotions:

This same law also applies to our emotions. If we are cross and irritable we send out such inharmonious vibrations that they affect all those around us, and tend to make them also cross and irritable toward us. In other words, *like produces like and we reap the results of what we sow* or send forth. Conversely, if we smile and send forth happy and cheerful radiations we receive the same kind in return. Ordinarily we smile because we feel harmonious and happy within, and we therefore naturally radiate those forces and reap like forces in return. *Just try it.*

States of Consciousness:

All our words and acts are expressions of states of our consciousness within. But many of these expressions are not the manifestation of definite thoughts consciously reasoned out and deliberately expressed. They are more often the expression of instinctive—often negative—emotions and habits of the animal-self which have become established *by our failure to train and discipline it* according to well-reasoned thoughts which express the high and constructive ideals which we have deliberately chosen and adopted as worthy of attainment and expression.

Lack of Training:

Because of this lack of emotional training and control we often express emotions which thought, reason and experience tell us are not wise, and which we would not

---

[4] *St. Matthew*, xii, 36.

express if we "only stopped to think." But since those who have not practiced self-control and self-discipline do not often "stop to think," but speak and act impulsively, their reaction is the spontaneous and instinctive expression of the characteristics of the untrained animal-self.

The Body not We:

We all know that the body is not we, the I Am. It is not the Real or Spiritual Self, but is only an animal into which we have temporarily projected our ray of consciousness in order that we may find expression through it and experience the conditions and learn the lessons of this temporary visit to the physical world. Therefore, without our proper training of this animal and its instinctive reactions, we cannot expect it to react in any other way than to its unreasoned instincts of self-preservation, self-aggrandizement and self-indulgence. And these instincts find expression largely through the negative and destructive emotions.

Animal Emotions:

When all goes well with the animal-self it is happy and contented, but when conditions arise which the animal fears will interfere with its welfare or habits or curb its self-indulgence, then opposition and negative emotions are at once aroused. These are sometimes useful and necessary for self-preservation, and such instinctive reactions are then justified by reason and common sense.

Fears:

But most of our words and acts which are aroused by fears of one sort or another (physical, moral, social, psychic) *are not justified* by reason or common sense. Especially is this true of such destructive emotions as anger, hatred, jealousy, envy, covetousness, etc. Once these are recognized as being *not our emotions* but those of the animal-self, the *absolute necessity* for self-discipline will be seen.

Self-discipline:

And self-discipline means training the animal-self to be governed, not by its animal instincts, but by the ideals and wisdom of the Real or Spiritual Being who is temporarily incarnated in the animal body and which It is striving to control and train for Its greater expression. It must be *trained to react* as automatically *to our ideals* as it formerly did to its animal instincts.

Practice Smiling:

The importance of this philosophical explanation is that our emotions are the most powerful sources of the radiations we send out, even more powerful than our thoughts and words, both of which are frequently dominated and changed by our emotions. How important it is, therefore, to *cultivate* our constructive emotions. One of the easiest ways to do this is to smile, to *deliberately practice smiling*. Ordinarily when we smile it is the natural outward expression of a friendly feeling we have within our hearts toward the one at whom we smile.

Friendliness:

Now, friendliness is but an early stage in the manifestation of love, or that divine harmony of the I Am within in which we should envelop all of God's creatures. Therefore, a true smile, *which must come from the heart*, will awaken a corresponding vibration in the one toward whom we radiate our smile. *Just try it.* And he will naturally react to it and express that same vibration back to us, unless some outside thought or emotion is allowed to step in to suppress it. As Milton tells us: "For smiles from reason flow, to the brute denied, and are of love the food."[5]

---
[5] *Paradise Lost*, Book viii, line 618.

The Spiritual Effect:

But the most important effect upon us of smiling is the psychological and spiritual one. Since a real smile must come from the heart, it sets a current of kindness and love flowing toward the one at whom we smile. This creates a *definite current* of spiritual magnetism which actually *envelopes* its object and *penetrates* his aura to his heart and *stimulates a like reaction.* And when we have charged ourselves with our current of positive friendliness, we are impervious to any negative reactions, such as a frown or an ungracious or sullen look or unfriendly reply.

Refuse to React:

And usually, if we consciously *refuse to react* to such negative responses but *intentionally keep on smiling* in the face of seeming rebuff, our current of friendliness and love will melt the opposition and secure a smile in return. *Just try it.* It is said that a continued smile and a hearty laugh, if not dissipated by fear, will even disarm and make harmless many wild animals.

Smiling Within:

This determination to maintain the *smiling feeling within* and to charge our whole personality with friendliness, acts so positively that we actually radiate our love-charged magnetism and thus develop both the love-radiating qualities in ourselves and increase our reliance upon them. And the more we habitually rely upon the love of the Divine Self within, and the more determinedly express that Self, the more nearly divine we become here on Earth. *Just try it.*

Effect on Others:

The next important effect of deliberately smiling is its result within the one smiled upon. The natural tendency is for one vibration to call forth and match another, a frown for a frown and a smile for a smile. Therefore, our smile tends to arouse a friendly response, and, more important still, to bring it into expression. Just as our hearts instinctively respond to a baby's cooing smile, and we say: "What a dear! Isn't it a darling? Don't you love it?" so does our fellow man tend to respond to our smile.

Help to Others:

Thus our smile will help him neutralize and throw off any vibration of gloom, irritation or unhappiness which may surround him and to which he may be reacting. Our smile, therefore, assists him to manifest the Divine in him, the love-aspect of his nature. Thus do we unconsciously contribute to his spiritual growth. *Just try it.*

How to Start the Day:

But the mere knowledge of this Law of Radiation and its reactions is of little value to us unless we *put it into practical operation.* Therefore, we should *form the habit of always starting the day with a smile.* If we do not feel much like smiling *we can induce that state.* For it is a psychological law that, "going through the motions tends to induce the same state which originally produced the motions." Understanding this law, many psychologists require their melancholic or nervous patients to stand before a mirror regularly the first thing every morning and wrinkle their faces into the form of a smile and study it to see that the result is a really friendly smile and not just a grimace. And soon they will be really smiling. *Just try it.*

A Practical Exercise:

Many students have asked for "something to do," some practical exercise for the mastery of self and the cultivation of spirituality, and here it is. Many expect some difficult form of concentration or yoga, but here is a simple little thing which, because of its very simplicity, is apt to be neglected, yet which is of the greatest practical importance. For few of us are naturally gifted with such a sunny disposition that we naturally smile our way through life. Hence s*miling needs to be cultivated* like musical or artistic ability or any other talent that is important to our culture, welfare, happiness and success.

The Prison House:

Many persons are so shut up in the prison house of self that they are actually ill because they cannot escape from their negative reactions. The muscles of their faces have become inflexible and set in ridges of tension. Their brows are wrinkled and furrowed with care or negative and depressing emotions whose lines become deeper and deeper as though cut in stone.

Muscular Habits:

Once fixed in this habit the muscles actually fight against any change of expression. It, therefore, requires will-power, determination and *persistent practice* to establish the new habit of smiling. When the corners of our mouths turn down, are relaxed and flabby, our spirits turn down with them. So we must *deliberately practice turning them up* so that we can smile at will, and even before we need to will it. *Just try it.*

Why We "Don't feel like it":

The more we "don't feel like it" the more we need it, and the more will-power and determination it requires. That is just the trouble, we do not *feel* like it. Why? Because we are not responding to the harmony and joy of the Divine Self within. We must, therefore, concentrate on that inner harmony, joy and love until we express and radiate it. Let us *make a definite exercise of it* while arranging our hair or while shaving, etc. *Just try it.*

Our Spiritual Toilet:

We give time and attention to completing our physical toilet before we appear in public And our spiritual toilet is just as important and is not complete without a smile. If we *start the day* with a positive smile and a laugh the rest of the day will take care of itself. *Just try it.* So, as soon as we awaken and say a prayer, such as the "Morning Prayer" or "Prayer for Light,"[6] and give thanks for our preservation through the night, we should *deliberately smile* with joy that we have been given another day in which to improve and increase and manifest more of our Real Self than we did the day before. We should realize that each day is a new incarnation, a new chance to take up our life expression again, a new opportunity to improve and perfect and radiate that expression.

Smile at Breakfast:

We should begin our self-discipline by making it a positive rule *never* to go down to the breakfast table *untill we can do so with a smile* which shall be so positive and dynamic that it will radiate our friendliness and love to one and all. Greet each one heartily and sincerely. When you say, "How are *you* this morning?" express real interest and concern that each may be well and happy. And if we smile positively and dynamically at each one we can start each one out for the day smiling also. *Just try it.*

Prepared Positively for the Day:

Starting out with this *positive radiation* we are properly primed to meet every condition, circumstance or test resolutely and harmoniously and can make the most of each incident; for smiling keeps us poised within and therefore self-controlled. *Just try it.* Thus we are able to carry on through any condition, because we are so

---

[6] See *Prayers of the O. C. M.*, Curtiss, 1, 3.

positively sustained by the radiations of our inner harmony that we can smile even in the face of adversity. *Just try it.* Especially *during the hot months*, when so many are tired, nervous and easily irritated, how refreshing and harmonizing is a cheerful smile when needed most! And in cold weather how warming is a cheery smile! *Just try it. Never miss a chance* to use it.

As the poet says:

> "Tis easy enough to be pleasant
> When life goes along like a song;
> But the man worth while is the one who will smile
> When everything goes dead wrong.
> For the test of the heart is trouble,
> And it always comes with the years,
> But the smile that is worth the praises of earth,
> Is the smile that comes through tears."[7]

Prevents Misunderstanding:

A real smile is not the silly giggle of an immature or vacant mind, but a real heart-radiation of dynamic power. Do not fail to use it at the critical moment. *Just try it.* When nonplussed or taken unawares, *smile before you speak*. It will affect your own mental state as well as the other person's, and will modify the reactions of both. It often thus obviates misunderstandings and avoids serious trouble. *Just try it.* No introduction to strangers is necessary if a cordial smile comes from the heart. It passes current among all peoples in all lands and in all ages. *Just try it.*

The Smile of God:

Once realize that all manifestation in Nature is but a part of the smile of God in creative expression, and we will do our best to help complete and perfect that expression by consciously radiating our own inner harmony and

---
[7] *Worth While*, Ella Wheeler Wilcox.

beauty as freely and as naturally as the smiling face of Nature does through the flowers, the trees and the songs of birds.

The Welcomed Smile:

If we all will practice smiling at everyone to whom we speak, and looking up with a smile at everyone who speaks to us, and giving a pleasant glance to everyone who glances at us, we will soon become known as "those happy, smiling people." And the cheer and happiness we thus radiate will make us welcome at any gathering and in all walks of life, as well as make ourselves happy, healthy and successful. So *smile, smile, smile! Just try it.*

CHAPTER IX

THE CLOUD UPON THE MOUNTAIN

Why the Effect:
When only results and manifestations are seen, they may seem to appear spontaneously and without previous preparation, but investigation will always show that the causes which operate to produce results invariably follow certain laws and methods of procedure. In other words, there is always a sequence of events and a mechanism by which the results are produced. Unless the details of the procedure follow in their proper sequence, the desired manifestation will not take place. This law applies to the mental, psychic and spiritual manifestations, which so puzzle us in the *Bible*, as well as to physical events.

Application:
Once we understand the method and the mechanism we can work in harmony with the law and produce the results more quickly and easily. It is to explain the methods used and the technique necessary to produce spiritual results that we present our Cosmic Soul Science, so that students may have a scientific explanation of the operation of the universal Law of Manifestation in the various events, and thus have a scientific and demonstrable basis for their religion and for their faith and belief.

All from the Invisible:
We are all familiar with that phase of the Law of Manifestation whereby all living things in the visible

world descend from the invisible and materialize on earth. The mechanism by which this is usually accomplished is through the slow Law of Growth. The archetype, ideal or mental pattern of all that is to manifest is projected by the Will of God into the super-physical or astral world.[1] There an astral pattern or model is formed, and from it there is projected into earth conditions — by a process of condensation and materialization — a germ, seed or egg embodying the potencies of the thing to be manifested. This acts as a focal point in matter through which the consciousness and life-force of the invisible being and its pattern or model can flow, and through which their constructive and cohesive powers slowly attract just those essences, forces, material conditions and physical particles which are needed to be built into the meshes of the astral pattern to materialize it.

Law of Growth:

This whole complicated and mysterious process we lightly, and quite unthinkingly, dismiss under the term growth or the Law of Growth. But growth is a relatively slow process, a process by which physical particles are gathered and built into the structure atom by atom, cell by cell, tissue by tissue. Therefore, all things that are to be normal and stable, that are to endure for their particular cycle of manifestation, must follow the slow Law of Growth.

Personal Effort Needed:

We sometimes become impatient when we do not seem to be progressing in spiritual realization and unfoldment as rapidly as we did when we first began definite study along these lines. But if we realize that we must follow the slow Law of Growth in our mental development as our consciousness gradually expands to grasp bigger ideas, and also in our spiritual growth as our realization deepens

---

[1] See Chapter VIII.

and broadens to enable us to respond to more spiritual realities, then we need not be impatient. For *no permanent attainment is gained except through personal effort* according to the slow Law of Growth.

New Lessons:

The rapid advance we made at first is due to the fact that we have been but reviewing old lessons learned in past lives through the slow Law of Growth. Hence we do not need to ponder and weigh and argue about them now. We know that which attracts us is true, and we understand it as soon as our attention is called to it. But a time soon comes when we have reviewed the old lessons learned in the past and must take up new lessons. These require time, study, meditation and effort to grasp and assimilate, according to the slow Law of Growth, if we are to build them into our consciousness, our character and our life.

Higher Laws:

When we read of how God manifested through marvelous phenomena to guide the Children of Israel, we usually think of such things as something separate and apart from ordinary life and law. But a little study will show that, while nearly all things in the material world materialize through the Law of Growth, there is a higher law and a phenomenal method used by higher Beings in the invisible when They desire to manifest temporarily for some reason that is so important and immediate that the slow method of materialization through growth will not do.

Materialization:

This is a method of condensation, etherealization and precipitation, utilizing much the same principle that the emanations of ectoplasm from the etheric double of a medium and the sitters at a séance are used to build up a semiphysical form or vehicle through which the intelligence and forces of discarnate beings can manifest.[2] This usually takes the form of a mist or cloud out of which the manifestation takes place. This cloud is composed partly of the condensation of higher forces and substances, but to produce *physical* results some of the finer materials and forces of man—also to some extent those of animals and plants—must be used, because the odic force of the higher Beings is far too fine and pure to manifest on Earth without being mixed with the coarser substances of terrestrial beings.

Psychical Phenomena:

Our *Bible* and the scriptures of other nations are full of accounts of such phenomenal manifestations of high spiritual Beings to man. Thus, when Jehovah wished to guide the Israelites out of Egypt He gathered up the animal magnetism, astral emanations and odic force of the multitude and their animals, together with whatever ectoplasm could be exuded by the priesthood and the more sensitive persons, and used it to help condense a visible pillar of cloud to lead them by day. (*Exodus*, xiii, 21). This condensed cloud formed a shell about Jehovah and gave Him a physical vehicle through which He could manifest to the physical senses of the multitude. "And the angel of God, which went before the camp of Israel, removed and went behind them: and (therefore) the pillar of cloud went from before their face, and stood behind." (*Exodus*, xiv, 19).

The Pillar of Fire:

If the cosmic force manifesting through the cloud is sufficiently powerful it will be visible in the dark as a glow, or if still more powerful, as a bright light. That is why the pillar of cloud became a pillar of fire at night. It must, therefore, have been at night when the angel of the

---
[2] For details see *Realms of the Living Dead*, Curtiss.

Lord first appeared to Moses "in a flame of fire out of the midst of a bush; and he looked, and, behold, the bush burned with fire (or glowed with spiritual radiance) and the bush was not consumed." (*Exodus*, iii, 2). Had this incident occured in the daytime Moses would have seen only a mist or small cloud about the bush. The bush was probably of the *shittah* or acacia family, as that wood has the purest and most powerful odic emanations, hence it would be easier for the communicating intelligence to manifest through the od of such a bush. Because of this exceptional quality of its odic force, only wood of the acacia tree was used in the building of the tabernacle.

Odic Force:

As we have pointed out elsewhere,[3] mountains are great sources of radiant odic force. It is therefore easier for the Masters from the higher realms to manifest on a mountain top, for there the odic forces of the earth are purest and freest from contamination by lower emanations and can thus more easily combine with the forces of the higher Beings to produce a cloud. At the time referred to in the text, the Israelites had only recently been released from slavery, hence they were an uneducated and nomadic people who required physical demonstrations of the reality and power of their divine guidance.

Laws are Unchanging:

Since the laws of the various forms of spirit communication are fixed and unchanging, they are the same in all races and in all ages. And just as a materializing medium requires a cabinet to condense the odic or astral forces to produce physical phenomena in a séance, so did Moses require a special tent, and later a permanent tabernacle, in which the odic forces from himself, the priesthood and the multitude could be condensed and purified and pre-

---

[3] *The Voice of Isis*, Curtiss, 312.

pared to mingle with corresponding forces poured down from above. "Odic force is the motive power throughout all God's creation as well as in the spirits' workshop on earth."[4]

Discarnate Mortals:

Discarnate mortals dwelling in the lower earth-bound realms of the astral world, when properly trained "over there," can use the odic forces and ectoplasm of a materializing medium to produce physical manifestations directly and with very little change, as such entities are dwelling very close to the earth plane. But advanced Souls who have passed through the state of purgatory and have been purged of the low earth magnetism, cannot use such low vibrating and contaminated, but only purified, ectoplasm. As Johannes Greber rightly says: "The odic power of a medium, although it may be sufficient in quantity, is not always fit for immediate use. It must first, in all cases in which it is to be employed by the 'superior world' as a motive force, be purified, or, so to speak, 'filtered.' To be sure, the *inferior spirit-world* need not undertake any purification of the od of the mediums, for the more impure this is, the better it is adapted to the od of such spirits. Hence it is also much easier for them to use such mediums for their purposes, and they arrive at this end much more quickly than do the *superior spirits*."[4]

The Independent Voice:

Later on, after these first public and physical demonstrations of His presence and power, when Jehovah wished to speak to Moses, the odic force and ectoplasm were concentrated by the spirit alchemists (the Cherubs) into a cloud above the Ark of the Covenant from which the spirit voice would then speak. "Then he heard the

---

[4] *Communication with the Spirit World*, Greber, 92-3.

voice of one speaking unto him from off the mercy seat that was upon the Ark of Testimony, from between the cherubims." (*Numbers*, vii, 89). "And the Lord spake unto Moses face to face, as a man speaketh unto his friend." (*Exodus*, xxxiii, 11).

Electrocution:

If the purified and powerful odic currents produced in the cabinet of the tent or tabernacle by the spirit alchemists were to come into contact with lower and impure currents, all that could not vibrate to the higher rates would be consumed. Hence the bearer of the impure currents would be practically electrocuted just as surely as if he had contacted a high-voltage power wire on earth. For this reason even the high priest Aaron was not permitted to enter the sanctuary until after the condensation had taken place and the high tension currents had been shut off. He was even required to call out that he had been able to contact the forces properly and was unharmed. "And his sound (voice) shall be heard when he goeth in unto the holy place before the Lord, and when he cometh out, that he die not." (*Exodus*, xxviii, 35). Such contact was dangerous unless properly done, for when Aaron's sons, Nadab and Abihu, "offered strange (that is, impure) fire before the Lord, *which he commanded them not*, there went out fire from the Lord, and devoured them, and they died before the Lord." (*Leviticus*, x, 1-2).

Reason for Darkness:

Since the human odic emanations and teleplasm or ectoplasm are *soluble in light*, most manifestations of them must take place in the dark. It therefore required tremendous cosmic currents of extremely high tension comparable to lightning to condense an ectoplasmic cloud in broad daylight out of which a materialized voice could speak loud enough for the multitude to hear. To produce physical phenomena in the light the cloud had to be very condensed or thick. "Lo, I come unto thee in a *thick* cloud, that the people may *hear* when I speak with thee and believe thee forever." (*Exodus*, xix, 9). Hence it was only on especially important occasions when demonstrations to all the multitude were to be made that they were done in the daylight on the mountain top.

Dangers Involved:

While the condensation was taking place the whole region was so dangerous that all but Moses and Aaron, who were properly trained to deal with those high currents, were forbidden to come near the place lest they die. "And thou shalt set bounds unto the people round about, saving, Take heed to yourselves, that ye go not up into the mount, or (even) *touch* the border of it: whoso *toucheth* the mount shall be surely put to death: there shall not a hand touch it." (*Exodus*, xix, 12).

Force of Metals:

Among minerals, the odic force of those which rust, disintegrate easily or tarnish badly have a destructive effect on the odic forces of the higher ethers. This is one of the reasons (there are others) why only gold, silver and copper were used in the tabernacle and temple service. Likewise the breastplate worn by the high priest before "enquiring of the Lord" contained twelve jewels selected because of the radio-active effect of their odic emanations.

Linen Garments:

For similar reasons the garments of the priests and other attendants, also the curtains, veils, altar-cloths, etc were of linen or byssus, the size of the thread and the fineness or coarseness of the quality varying according to the purpose for which it was used. The rank of the priests could therefore easily be told by the quality of the garments. "And thou shalt put upon them linen breeches.... when they come in unto the tabernacle (tent of meeting) of the congregation, or when they come near unto the altar to minister in the holy place; that they bear not iniquity (or impurity) and die." (*Exodus*, xxviii, 43).

Effect of Colors or Odors:

Because of their odic radiations, only certain colors were used in the temple service, such as blue, purple, scarlet, white and gold. The ephod or robe donned by the high priest when entering the sanctuary was of blue linen embroidered alternately with golden balls and purple pomegranates. (*Exodus*, xxviii, 4). For similar reasons all the details of the construction, furnishings and utensils of the temple were carefully specified in detail. (*Exodus*, xxxi). "And the Lord said unto Moses, take unto thee sweet spices, stacte, and onycha and galbanum; these sweet spices with pure frank-incense. . . . And thou shalt make it a perfume, a confection after the art of the apothecary, tempered together, pure and holy. . . . for the Lord." (*Exodus*, xxx, 34-7).

Physical Demonstrations:

Through all these means the Progenitor of the Race, Jehovah, and His deputies, the angelic messengers or tribal gods, the spiritual guardians of the various tribes, were able to give demonstrations of their presence and power which were of such an overwhelming *physical* character as to impress the undeveloped minds of the ignorant multitude and ensure their obedience.

Power of the Voice:

So powerful were the super-physical cosmic currents required, that the vibrations of the voice were "stepped up" to an enormous degree so that the whole multitude could hear them, just as by the proper use of a microphone and a loud speaker the sound of heart-beat can be made to fill the room, or the friction of the joints can be heard as a loud, harsh squeek. Thus the voice was made to reverberate like thunder, and even shook the trees and made the people tremble. Therefore, it was literally true and scientifically accurate to say: "God *thundereth* marvelously with His voice," (*Job*, xxxvii, 5). "The voice of the Lord is powerful.... The voice of the Lord *breaketh the cedars*.... The voice of the Lord *shaketh the wilderness*." (*Psalms*, xxxix, 4-8).

The Voice of God:

On one occasion it required three days to generate the necessary force. "And it came to pass on the *third* day in the morning, that there were thunderings and lightnings, and a *thick* cloud upon the mount, and the voice of a *trumpet* (or megaphone) exceeding *loud*; so that *all the people* that was in the camp *trembled*." (*Exodus*, xix, 16). Thus, from ancient times thunder has been connected with the voice of God. Formerly this was considered very mysterious, and has even been called "mere superstition," but now that we understand the mechanism we see that under the conditions given the thunderous voice was a *physical reality*, scientifically produced according to the now well-known laws of electrical vibrations.

The Druids:

Before the final sinking of the continent Atlantis beneath the Atlantic ocean, a large colony of priests of the White Brotherhood and their followers migrated to what are known as the British Isles, and became the ancestors of the Druids. For ages these were the most learned and cultured people of Europe, and were the progenitors or source of the later culture of both Egypt and Greece. From their center they sent out missionaries and established branch colonies in seven principal countries. According to Stinson Jarvis the seven branches of the Druid Church were named after the seven stars of the Pleiades. "The constellation was at the center of the priestly heavens, and had the most honorable position in the neck of the constellation Taurus, the Bull, who represented the BULL and *Thunder-god* of England."[5] England is still called "John Bull," the animal whose bellow rumbles like thunder.

Role of Thunder:

One of the Druid legends says that God gave to a woman a large cask called a TUN, and after the spigot was opened it could not be closed, and from the leakage came all the rivers of the world. "In England Father Thames is still pictured as sitting astride a large cask or TUN, from which water trickles.... The great booming Land-Shaker (Thunderer) was named upon the hollow booming sound of the empty TUN when it was rolled."[6] The poet Homer says that Nep-TUN, the God of the waters, lived on the Thames, which was regarded as the father of all rivers.

The "Thunderer":

It is no wonder then that London, on the river Thames, still rules the physical sea through its navy, as the Druid Church once ruled the seas of humanity through her branch churches which gave out her thunderous decrees as "the Voice of God." Since the Druid Priests were regarded as "the mouthpiece of God," they were called the "Thunderers," and their decrees inspired almost as much awe and obedience as did the thunderous voice of Jehovah from the thick cloud upon the mountain top. And even today the most influential paper in England, the *London Times*, is called the "Thunderer" since it is supposed to speak with such authority. Thus is England identified with thunder and hence symbolized heaven.

---

[5] *The Key to the Universe*, Curtiss, 275.
[6] *The Price of Peace*, Jarvis, 56-55.

Orders Issued:

Because of its white chalk cliffs, England is still called Alb-in or Alb-ion, meaning the White Island, from the root *alba* meaning white. Thus again heavenly messages of spiritual teachers, also political orders, were issued as "the thunder of God."

Mount of the Law:

Since God spake to the Israelites from the cloud upon the mountain, the white cloud, also white snow upon the mountains, is used as a symbol, both of the dwelling place and the cold, impersonal purity of the decrees of God. The cloud-capped mountain therefore symbolizes both the authority and the power of God's will as expressed through law. Since the judges of the highest court of England are supposed to ascertain the exact truth and to administer the will of God as expressed through law—as the Druid priests actually did through their psychic and spiritual communion with Him—the judges in England to this day still wear a full white wig to symbolize the white cloud upon the Mount of the Law which they represent and by which they should be inspired. Hence their decisions have the authority of the voice of God whose representatives they are supposed to be to administer His justice.

Symbology:

The cloud upon the mountain is therefore an universal symbol of the direct, phenomenal and *physical* manifestation of God to man through psychic or odic power, the thunder representing His voice and the lightning the flashes of His eyes when "angry," that is, when the people resist His guidance. Those who say that *all* use of psychic forces is evil, and that God and other spiritual forces do not manifest through psychic powers, simply do not know their *Bibles*, and are simply stating their own untutored and unsupported opinion.

The Real Self:

Applying this universal symbology to our personal lives, the cloud upon the mountain symbolizes the cloud of glory radiated by our own Real or Divine Self from the higher realms, or from the top of the Mount of Attainment. With the great mass of mankind that great cloud of spiritual radiance is much like the dot over the little letter i, which represents the little human personality: that is, it is just an overshadowing of the loving I Am Presence. But as we send up our currents of aspiration to attain the spiritual heights, we gradually reach up toward that Divine Dot until finally we merge the little i into it and become one with it, and so become the capital I of the I Am Presence. Then we can say with Jesus: "I and my father are 1." But we can accomplish this only as we open our hearts to the light and love of the over-shadowing cloud of glory, and through prayer and definite times of meditation, ask the Voice of God within to guide us through the wilderness of material existence to the Promised Land of spiritual realization and attainment.

CHAPTER X

ALL CONQUERING LOVE

A Satisfactory Solution:

In the swiftly changing conditions of modern life there is a pathetic eagerness among all classes for some basic principle upon which they can rely and by the application of which they can solve their problems and attain the peace and happiness so necessary to their progress. But to search for such a panacea in the outer world is utterly fruitless, because the outer visible world is the world of effects, not of origins; of results, not of causes. To seek for it in the mental world is to encounter countless theories created by the intellectual speculations of the human mind throughout the ages, which upon trial do not meet the requirements for constructive and concrete results. Therefore, the only hope of a satisfactory solution is to seek in the inner World of Causation for some cosmic principle of expression which is fundamental to all manifestation. Such a fundamental cosmic principle we find in Divine Love.

The Mother-force:

While the mighty creative Father-force of Divine Will is that which projects the ideal of the manifested universe into expression, it is the tremendous creative Mother-force of Divine Love that cherishes that ideal, nourishes and brings it forth. Hence, it is to Divine Love that you must look, to bring forth your ideals of life. But first you must realize that we are not mere mortals, but Divine

Beings, "heirs of God, and joint-heirs with Christ." Consequently, you have all the powers of God the Father-Mother to draw upon to help you in the manifestation of your divinity.

Realization Needed:

You must therefore seek earnestly and ardently for a realization of what Divine Love is. You must feel it as a warm radiance which spreads out over the whole universe, bringing to every person, every creature and every thing upon the Earth the mighty joy of living, of growing, of *expressing its ideal*,—of accomplishing and attaining the object for which each was put forth into manifestation. Once this realization has been gained, you can begin to use it in your life. For you will then understand that the inner radiance of this Divine Love is forever pouring forth through you from its center of light, the loving I Am Presence or Christ-consciousness within, and is flooding your whole being and all your activities and affairs with its creative and regenerative and perfecting power.

Symbology of Water:

Water is the symbol universally used to indicate the Divine Mother-force of love. And as water is the most universal solvent and cleanser known to man in the outer life and world, so is Divine Love the universal solvent and cleanser in the inner life and world. There is no thought, desire or ambition that, if subjected to a current of Divine Love, will not be purified and have its dross of earth dissolved and washed away; no emotion that will not be purged of its selfishness and negative vibrations; no problem or obstacle to your welfare and spiritual advance that will not be disintegrated, dissolved and so disappear from your path of life if you consciously and continually bathe it in the penetrating power of Divine Love.

God-in-Action:

Remember that this cosmic force of Divine Love is not a mere intellectual concept or metaphysical speculation, but is a mighty dynamic, cosmic, electronic force which you can wield consciously to attain definite ends if you will. It is literally *God-in-action*. But it will never force itself upon you or compel you to use it. It will never descend to manifest outwardly until it is first invited and invoked to manifest within and through you. And there is but one method of invoking it, and that is through your eager aspiration, your sincere love for and your fervent prayer for and devotion to it.

Your Radiation:

Once you have realized this Divine Love of the Christ within as a blazing white light so intense that you actually *feel it* thrilling and illuminating, warming and vitalizing you and *radiating from you*, then it will begin to accomplish its miracles for you. *Stop now* and *meditate upon it* that it may bring you the realization that Divine Love is truly God-in-action in your heart, in your mind, in your body, and in all your affairs.

At Your Command:

Knowing that it is responsive to your direction, you can command it to surge through your body, penetrating and bathing every cell with its cleansing power, washing out all impurities and revitalizing every tissue and organ until every function is restored to normal and you manifest perfect, radiant and joyous health.[1] Then turn the current of this Divine Love into your mind, dissolving all negative or limiting ideas, all resistance to new and higher concepts of life and love, leaving your mind calm and receptive to inspiration and guidance from above.

---

[1] Of course you must cease creating the causes of ill health, such as wrong food combinations, faulty elimination, inharmonious thoughts, destructive emotions, etc. For details see *Four-Fold Health*, Curtiss.

Purified Emotions:

Then turn it into your emotions, washing away all irritation, all antagonism toward, or envy or jealousy of, others, leaving your feelings poised and quiescent and at sweet peace with all the world. If you have reason to believe that anyone is inharmonious or antagonistic toward you, *do not resist* or fight back, but simply bathe that one with wave after wave of the white Christ-love and see all his or her opposition dissolved and washed away, leaving only peace and harmony. If there is some material, physical problem, condition or obstacle that seems to block the path of your progress, focus your thought upon it and bathe it and all connected with it in the warm current of the Christ-love and you will see the opposition rapidly crumble and disappear or you will be shown how to solve the problem.

A Criminal's Vision:

A number of beautiful examples of this use of the Loveforce are given in a recent book entitled *Love Can Open Prison Doors*, by Starr Daily, which illustrates the working of this law so exactly and practically that it is worth quoting extensively. The author was a hardened, habitual criminal who had deliberately violated his parole and had been returned to serve out a full twenty-year sentence. After spending many days in solitary confinement in a dark, damp "dungeon hole," hating God, himself and everything else, he had a miraculous vision of the Master Jesus. He was so surrounded and utterly filled with the Master's Divine Love that it dissolved all his hatreds and purged him from his impurities. Some hours afterward he says: "Where I had been the *recipient* of the Master's Love, I now felt myself *exuding* love. It seemed to pour from me in the form of a mighty sense of blissful gratitude, not for any one thing, but for all things, for life. I had no discernment or consciousness apart from this enchantment of love. . . .

A Dungeon Illumined:

"There was no sensibility of discomfort attached to the dungeon now, no feeling of bitterness. The place seemed to radiate with a wholly congenial and alluring atmosphere. . . . Unusual things began to happen. The prison doctor stopped at my door *for the first time*, to enquire after my health, and to linger and talk. . . . The keeper of the dungeon, a man who had taken a violent dislike to me from the first, came to my door with gracious words on his lips. I had hated him and now I loved him. . . . the deputy warden, who had been making regular daily visits to my door, suddenly stopped coming. . . . on the third day he opened my door and said: 'Well, buddy, I think you've had enough. You can go over to the hospital and clean up and rest for a while'. . . . a few days later I was assigned a new and easier job in the prison shirt shop.

Changing Old Habits:

"My problems were many and of life long duration. . . . My intention was to go to war against them and slay them in one fell blow with the rapier of my will. . . . The more I tried to war against my habits, the more persistently they pressed their claims upon me. . . . A sense of weakness and hopelessness took hold of me, which *defied constructive thinking*, which defied *thinking* of *any* kind, except thoughts of impotence and misery. . . . It seemed that all the legions of hell had turned out to concentrate their fire upon me alone. . . . I achieved (success) not by trying to suppress old habits, but by using life's creative law to *create new habits* that transcended the old.

The Futility of Fighting:

"To war against a thing is to hate that thing. To sublimate a condition is to employ the medium of love. The one intensifies the condition into a more intensified circumference, the other expands it until it has no circumference left. . . . the easiest and safest way to rid yourself of many bad habits is to recondition yourself to one good habit. . . . I would analyze my thoughts as they drifted through my mind. If it was destructive, I would counter with a constructive one *deliberately created* for the purpose. . . . Reform is a matter of transcending old desires and habits of life, not by suppression of them through fear or other forces. So long as the habits are not risen above, a relapse into them is constantly immanent. . . .

Constructive Deeds:

"Then I hatched up another game. . . . of constructive *deeds*. Each day I tried to increase the number of little unobtrusive things I could do for my fellows. . . . *in every case* I was rewarded by seeing the iceberg melt that had stood between us, and it wasn't long until I had no enemies left. . . . It was an expanding something that drew men closer to me. . . . (When the prison chaplain disapproved of advanced-thought literature and prevented it from reaching him). My first impulse was to fly into a good old fashioned fit of rebellion and write the chaplain a vituperative note of denunciation. . . . (then) I began to think of him in terms of *brotherly love* and to *feel what I thought* intensely. Then one day at noon he came. . . . with several magazines that had been sent me. He had seen fit to censor them. . . . (but) he had changed his mind. This *demonstration of the power of love* to use creative principle effectively against adverse conditions, not only helped me, but scores of my fellows, because shortly after it the chaplain lifted his ban. Obviously love can open—all manner of prison doors.

A Striking Demonstration:

"The case of Emmet Edwards comes to mind. . . . At the time I singled him out. . . . his face was drawn

All Conquering Love

and sallow, his eyes were hollow with black circles around them. . . . He was emaciated and his mind was already touched with feebleness. . . . For about a week I treated Emmet silently with the constructive thoughts of love. . . . By and by the influence of love acting upon the creative principle, began to have the desired effect. . . . In three months' time. . . . he became director of all prison athletics. . . . From a craven coward and a physical wreck, Emmet had climbed to the peak of courage.

Character Changed:

"In the tuberculosis ward was a patient known as Poison Jasper. For months he had been wasting away. As a patient he was the most ungovernable in the ward. As a man his heart was as bitter and black as any heart could be. . . . He cursed the God in whom he had never believed. . . . I had taken up a position at the foot of Jasper's bed. . . . looking down at him and reasoning in my heart that I stood before a potential Christ. . . . *This feeling consumed me* as I stood there. . . . From that moment on until Jasper's hour to go arrived, there was no more trouble with him.

Education Installed:

"When I first thought of asking the warden for the privilege of taking a course of study, I was fully aware that such a request would be flatly rejected. . . . How am I going to reach the warden? How am I going to make my love known to him?. . . . it grew and grew as I continued to search his inner being for the Christ-like traits that are the heritage of every human being. Finally, I began to visualize him in all manner of constructive humanitarian activities. . . . I saw him with the request in his hand. . . . As I watched him reading it, I let my love close in around him until he seemed to be completely enveloped in it. . . . I bowed in inward gratitude. . . . as he determined to allow me to have my course of study. . . . Today this prison has one of the finest educational systems in operation.

Sentence Shortened:

"My rating was not only that of an habitual criminal. My criminological rating had me listed as abnormal, *criminally insane*, incurably anti-social. I was hopelessly beyond the influence of reformation. The warden told me no power on earth could shorten my sentence one minute. . . . What I did, therefore, was to visualize the chairman in his favorite chair in his study. . . . I surrounded him with an atmosphere of peace, contentment, comfort, receptiveness. I talked to him with my thoughts, wishing him well. . . . For several months I kept faithfully and patiently at the experiment, not once allowing myself to become discouraged in the face of the fact that nothing seemed to happen. . . . Then I was called up before the board again, this time to receive my freedom. . . . *five years in advance* of the time fixed by law.

Love Must Direct:

"Always love causes something to be created. But always *love must direct* the creative principle toward constructive ends. . . . For the creative principle creates that which it is directed to create. That is its nature. And that is what it does. . . . The mother who loves her child so much that she relieves it of self-developing effort, is not loving constructively. . . . If every man would pause to question the course his desires were taking, and change that course if it be found destructive, this old world would soon notice a mighty falling off of misery."

You Can Conquer:

If the realization of the love of the Christ within, and the conscious direction of that Divine Love to his terrible and seemingly hopeless problems could work such miracles for a hopelessly hardened criminal, it can work just as great miracles in *your* life if you will *take the time to realise and use it* as he did. Your consciousness is your world, your universe. Nothing can enter it which you do not permit to enter it by responding to it. Therefore, you must choose that to which you wish to respond—the outer or the inner.

The Source of Power:

Remember that there is but one ultimate Source of all power, intelligence and love, and that is God. As we said before, all manifestations of life, consciousness and power are God-in-action. And He is in action in you. He manifests through the Christ-center of your heart. To conquer, you must first enter into the heart of your inner world and be still before the majestic Presence of your real Divine Self, the loving I Am Presence, and correlate with and then direct your current of Divine Love to solve all your problems.

Love is Irresistible:

Realize that Divine Love is a limitless, all-powerful, irresistible, divine energy which transcends all human concepts, but which has a focal point in you, and its current in you is subject to your control. By your conscious recognition of and correlation with it you can release this dynamic God-power to work its miracles in your life. Since it is the source of all health, all happiness, all supply and all perfection, when you recognize any lack of these qualities you should *refuse to react* to that lack or give it power over you. Immediately focus upon the negative conditions the all-conquering current of Divine Love and fill them with its *power of perfect manifestation*. See that perfection as already manifesting and refuse to think of anything less than perfection.

The Source of Happiness:

There can be no real happiness in the world without some manifestation of love. Since you reap only what you sow, if you do not receive expressions of love from those around you in the world without, then you are not radiating love to them from within. To "Love thy neighbor as thyself" you must first respond to that Divine Love that is within you, then it will flow forth to all the "neighbors" that you contact. You do not have to love the imperfections of their personalities. You merely bathe them in Divine Love until the imperfections are lost to sight in the radiance of Love; until the Divine Love within them is released to transmute them and shine out through the personality.

Love Your Enemies:

With this concept in mind you can understand the scientific principle back of the injunction to, "Love your enemies, bless (radiate to) them that curse you, do good to them that hate you, and pray for them that despitefully use you, and persecute you." You now see this injunction as a practical direction as to how to use Divine Love in a definite way. For by following this rule all enmity, antagonism, hatred and persecution are *disintegrated* and *consumed* by the radio-active power of Divine Love. And as the mighty current of Love is poured forth to such persons, none of their lesser currents can swim toward you or enter your aura against that mighty outgoing stream, and hence they cannot reach you.

The New Cycle:

We seem to be passing through a racial cycle of darkness, during times which may seem to become worse, when there is much sorrow, poverty, disappointment, suffering and despair. But as practical followers of the Christ we know that the night is far spent and that a new day, a new era, a new dispensation, a New Age is here. Therefore, each enlightened Soul has a great opportunity, a great duty, *a great responsibility* for spreading the realization and the radiations of Divine Love. You must *demonstrate* to the world that you are so conscious of the Divine Love within that it flows forth from you as a powerful protecting radiance which disintegrates all inharmonies and obstacles, and gives you perfect protection and also the power to face every outer and inner condition and pass triumphantly through it.

Demonstrate Your Divinity:

When you have realized, *definitely and intensely*, that you are not a mere mortal, but a Divine Being: when you have realized your power to reach up and contact the very throne of God, to become one with Him, to feel His omnipotent power filling you, His Divine Love enfolding you and His blessings showering down upon you, then you will be able to demonstrate your Divinity and manifest your perfection under all conditions.

His Helpers:

The enlightening and uplifting of humanity is a mighty, mighty task for the Christ to accomplish. And it can be accomplished only through those individuals who recognize Him and become one with Him and so become focal points on Earth through whom He can pour His force of Divine Love and Wisdom. When you have recognized this mighty Love that is waiting within you for expression and have *released it* in your life, then you can dwell in that God-consciousness and radiate the transmuting and all-conquering power of Divine Love to perform its miracles in your affairs.

Realization Needed:

Mere words cannot describe or express it. Only spiritual experiences can bring it to your realization. But once it has thrilled your heart and has sent its waves of Divine Fire coursing through the blood of your body: once it has lifted your consciousness into the realms of heavenly consciousness far above the things of Earth, then will your mind be illumined, and your adoration and aspiration will bring you into conscious oneness with Divine Love and ultimately bring forth in your heart the manifestation of the Christ within and make you a blessing to all you contact.

This is not merely a pleasing theory. It is a time-tested *method of applying* a universal law. Try it and prove it by faithfully applying it in your own life, and note the results.

Prayer for World Peace[1]

O Thou glorious Source of all life, light and love, our Lord God almighty! from whose heart the Ray of Spirit in each mortal is sprung! let the realization of our oneness in Thee descend upon our hearts as heavenly dew, refreshing our souls.

May the love of God and the fellowship of all mankind—without regard to race, creed or condition—so fill our hearts and minds that each will gladly unite his forces for the attainment of peace, fellowship and co-operation.

May all persons and classes and nations *cease their conflicts*, and unselfishly strive for peace and good-will, that world peace may speedily be attained.

Let the calm of Thy eternal peace, which passeth all intellectual understanding, envelop us with its divine serenity. May it quiet the turmoil of our minds, and the conflict of our desires, dissolve our fears, and reveal to us the essential brotherhood of all mankind.

Thus shall the power of Thy loving Spirit bring victory over all opposition to the establishment of Thy peace on earth, and good-will among mankind. Amen.

---

[1] From *The Philosophy of War*, Curtiss, 16, 17.

CHAPTER XI

THE HEAVEN WORLD

Co-Workers:

Jesus said that our true brothers and sisters are those who are of the same household of faith. Therefore, our common interest in the fact of survival and the demonstration of communion with those who have passed on, make us co-workers in the spread of that truth, no matter how far apart we may live.

Personal Survival:

Personal Survival is a fact in Nature, *scientifically proved*. It does not depend upon man's belief or his religion. Materialists and atheists will survive whether they believe it or not and whether they are good, bad or indifferent. Since the physical proofs of this fact have been recorded in countless volumes, we do not need to take up your time in presenting further proofs.

Basis of Religion:

The reality of the unseen world about us has been recognized in all ages. And the fact that there are unseen powers and conscious beings in the invisible with whom we can communicate is testified to in our own Christian scriptures and in all others. And this survival and communication is the basis of all religions and all forms of worship. Such forms of worship may vary from the lowest fetish and voodoo worship, in which artificially created astral elementals or "diakas" have to be propitiated and fed by the shedding of blood, up to the highest forms of initiation, realization and union with the Divine. All depend upon the reality of our contact with the invisible worlds. But in the Christian world, after the fifth century, such direct, conscious contact with the unseen ceased to be systematically practiced and gradually came to be frowned upon and finally banned.

Spiritual Hunger:

It remained for psychic research not only to demonstrate that fact, but to organize it into a form of practice and worship. But for one's own inner spiritual growth and progress it is not enough merely to demonstrate the fact of personal survival as a scientific law of Nature. Its physical demonstration may satisfy the intellectual requirements of a logical mind, and certainly should dispel all uncertainty and fear, and allay grief over the loss of our loved ones. But that is not enough. For man has more than a mind to satisfy. He has a heart also. And that heart hungers for the spiritual food of love and *a realization of God as a personal experience*, just as the mind hungers for the intellectual food of logical explanations of laws and phenomena of the world we see around us. Hence, something more than mere physical demonstration is necessary for complete Soul-satisfaction. A higher contact is necessary.

Biblical Phenomena:

As we pointed out in a previous chapter, the Children of Israel were given astounding physical demonstrations of psychic phenomena, from "the pillar of cloud by day and the pillar of fire by night" (*Exodus*, xiii, 21), the direct, independent voice "from off the mercy seat" (*Exodus*, xxxiii, 11) and "the voice of a trumpet exceeding loud: so that all the people that was in the camp trembled" (*Exodus*, xix, 16), a voice which spoke "face to face, as a man speaketh unto his friend," a voice so powerful that it "breaketh the cedars. . . . (and) shaketh the wilderness" (*Psalms*, xxxix, 4, 8). They were also given examples of levitation and the bodily transportation of living prophets through the air to distant places (apportation) (I *Kings*, xviii, 12; *Ezekiel*, iii, 14 and viii, 3) and the materialization of "the fingers of a man's hand, and wrote over against the candlestick upon the plaster of the wall of the king's palace: and the king saw the part of the hand that wrote" (*Daniel*, v, 5), and many other remarkable phenomena.

Phenomena Insufficient:

But all these marvelous phenomena did not keep them from backsliding or from building a golden calf (*Exodus*, xxxii, 4) and worshipping idols (*Isaiah*, ii, 8). Why? Because the mere phenomena, even though far exceeding in magnitude anything of modern times, did not touch their hearts and develop love, unselfishness, devotion and true heart-worship of God. They served in awe and fear rather than in love. Hence, those stupendous phenomena did not contribute to their true spiritual growth and did not greatly change the thoughts and habits of their daily lives. A higher realization was necessary.

Effect on Lives:

To be practical, let us apply this same test to ourselves individually. To what extent have psychic phenomena modified our lives after the wonder of the demonstrated continuity of life has worn off? How have they changed our habits? Have they made us more honest in the little things of daily life? Have they made us more patient, more tolerant of the faults and failings of others; more kind and loving to all we meet? Or do our lives go on in pretty much the same old way? If they do, then we need a higher realization; something that will develop *the Spirit within us*; something that will help us to live a more spiritual or even saintly life.

Saints:

Now, a saint is not necessarily one who has fully attained mastery, as the history of many medieval saints clearly shows. A saint is one whose love of God and whose desire for truth and righteousness cause him consciously to strive for a greater realization and expression of the love of God. He is one who lets God take charge of and control his *daily life and all his affairs*. He may still make mistakes at times, but he is ever ready to acknowledge them, to repent and strive to correct them. And by such striving to let the love of God shine forth in all his thoughts, words and deeds, he grows closer to God and to his fellow men, both in the seen and in the unseen. This is the result of true spiritual, rather than mere psychic, unfoldment.

Demonstration:

Physical demonstration is indeed as necessary and perfectly proper in its place today, as it was in the early Christian church; in fact, it is the scientific basis upon which our higher understanding of the seen as well as the unseen worlds is built. But *there is nothing spiritual* in mere scientific demonstration of personal survival. Again we say that a higher spiritual contact is necessary.

Life Hereafter:

You are all familiar with the fact that both scientific investigation and the countless reports from the unseen show that for a number of years after passing over, life in the lower astral world[1] is but a continuation or extension of the life here on earth. Those who leave the earth-plane have simply taken off their outer garments of flesh like an overcoat, and gone one flight up. But by so doing they do not raise their consciousness sufficiently or develop sufficient Divine Love to become bright and shining angels.

---
[1] For details see *Realms of the Living Dead*, Curtiss.

The Heaven World

Neither do they suddenly become all-wise. *They are just the same mortals* that they were here *until* they have progressed after arriving "over there." Hence, their judgment and their opinions given through their messages are not always wise or dependable.

Thoughts Still Rule:

It is true that those who have lived sincere and good lives here do not remain in the lower earth-bound realms, but find themselves in a far more beautiful world than this, but still a sublimated counterpart of earth conditions. They are still interested in much the same things and have much the same thoughts and desires. And they will remain so *until they listen to and follow* the higher teachers over there, and turn their attention from earthly to heavenly things, and are purged from their earthly vibrations. Only as they consciously seek higher ideals and aspire to spiritual attainments through love of God can they progress spiritually; for *merely passing from earth* into the unseen world *does not confer spirituality*. Otherwise discarnate criminals, drunkards and the insane would immediately enter heavenly conditions, and we know they do not.

Purgatory:

The Catholic Church rightly calls this first stage of the afterlife "purgatory." For in some phase of it we all must remain until we are purged from the vibrations, thoughts and desires which hold us down to earth conditions. In fact, often for years, thousands who have strong earth desires do not realize that they have left the earth-plane, as the researches of Dr. Wickland[2] and others have amply proved. Only as their rates of vibration are raised can they rise to the higher realms of light and happiness. And only after they have passed through the

---
[2] *Thirty Years Among the Dead*, Wickland.

"second death"—the death of the personality, but not the individuality—and have advanced beyond the astral world can they enter the real spiritual or heaven world, far above the astral.

Spirit Messages:

It is obvious that if our friends know about our conditions and affairs here on Earth, they must stay in close touch with us. It is only natural that for some time after passing over they should be intensely interested in our affairs, but after they have progressed to higher levels they must come down to earth-conditions to look into such matters for us. My mother and father say they cannot tell me much about my physical affairs without getting someone who is close to Earth to look into them and report, as it is difficult for them to come down and take on those earth-vibrations. Hence, if we ask our friends only material questions we hold them down to material levels. Therefore, when communicating with them we should ask questions of a spiritual nature: about how they are progressing over there and how they see we can progress down here. Then they are not held down to earth-conditions. It often happens that through our studies and aspirations we are farther advanced spiritually than our departed friends. And since those who are interested in us follow our thoughts and interests, *we are a great help to them* in their progression. Many on the other side of life attend our lectures, and we have often been told by them how much they have thus been helped.

Psychic Faculties:

Although most Spiritualists call the astral world the "spirit world" until they learn its limitations and its true relation to the higher worlds above it, we have shown that it *is not the true spiritual world*; nor are psychic faculties spiritual faculties, any more than our intellectual faculties are spiritual faculties. Neither do they take our consciousness into the spiritual world, but only into the astral world. Neither are they latent faculties which all will develop after death. *Psychic faculties* are merely the use of *our five senses* in the *astral world.* Hence these limited faculties cannot take our consciousness higher than the astral world, any more than our mental faculties can take us higher than the mental world, until those faculties have reached up to the spiritual world and been illumined by the down-pouring of the radiance of that world, far above the astral and next above the mental.

Spiritual Growth:

The question now arises, what constitutes spiritual growth? Our spiritual growth is determined by the degree of our realization of, and our personal contact with, God. And our contact with God is determined by the character of our heart's aspiration, our love for the true, the beautiful and the good. And we have already shown[3] that the only reasonable object of our presence here on Earth is in the growth of our consciousness of what is the Supreme Good which men call God, and our correlation with and expression of it.

Begin Here:

Research has shown that our departed friends are in no closer contact with God over there than when they were here, except to the degree that they have aspired to and sought *and attained* such contact since passing over. For the mere passing over does not bring us into the presence of God or the Christ. Therefore, we must begin our contact with Him here and now, whether we are psychically developed or not. For we do not have to wait until after death to begin that contact. This we can do through the higher realization of God or our Ray of His Spirit, the loving I Am Presence, within us now.

---

[3] See Chapters I and II.

What to Do:

But just how do we go about making our contact with God? Not through psychic phenomena, as said before, nor by the cultivation of psychic faculties, but through *higher aspiration*; through personal seeking for a *greater realization and worship* of God. As you questioned the effect of psychic phenomena upon yourself, what effect does the possession of psychic powers have on those who possess them? Unless they seek the higher contact, do they, as a rule, live more spiritual lives than other seekers for truth? Does possession of psychic gifts, great as these gifts are, make them known as outstanding examples of those qualities that come from true spiritual growth? Are they notably more loving and kind, more unselfish, more healthy and happy than those who have no psychic gifts? *Certainly not*, unless they seek *spiritual* unfoldment as well as psychic, and *live it* in their personal lives.

Results:

Have their psychic powers enabled them to accomplish results at all comparable to those attained by such spiritually unfolded Souls as George Fox, John Wesley, General Booth, Mrs. Eddy and the late Rev. Dick Sheppard, for example? If not, why not? Because, we repeat, the *astral world is not the spiritual world* nor the source of spiritual power. Hence contact with it alone does not bring *spiritual* power nor produce *spiritual* growth. It is true that all those mentioned above had a certain amount of psychic unfoldment, but what a difference in the use they made of it and what they added to it! Spiritualist churches often complain of their lack of growth and progress. The reason is easily seen. *Many* do not contact the heaven world, the *source of power and supply*, but only the astral world.

Consolation:

In these remarks we are not belittling mediums nor psychic powers nor their invaluable service to sorrowing humanity. We fully appreciate, because we have experienced it and know, the wonderful consolation and the joy that comes to people *on both sides of the grave* through such faculties. For in many instances such communication is of the utmost help to the discarnate one as well as to the enquirer. For instance, my mother tells me that my love for her bathes her in a warm current of spiritual force which helps her to advance every time I communicate with her, and especially when I pray for her.

St. Paul's Experience:

You will also remember that St. Paul communicated with the discarnate Jesus constantly, for he tells us: "But I certify you, brethren, that the gospel which was preached of me is not after man. For I neither received it of man, neither was I taught it, but it came to me through the revelation of Jesus Christ." (*Galatians*, i, 11, 12). Even Jesus communed with Moses and Elias (*Matth.*, xvii, 3), and often went apart to commune with the higher realms, or heaven world.

Spiritual Power:

We do not belittle proper communications with the astral world. We are only trying to make you think, to differentiate, to discriminate between astral and spiritual powers; as to where spiritual power comes from and how it is attained. All the great spiritual teachers and leaders throughout the ages no doubt possessed psychic powers, but *they added something more important* to their use, namely, *spiritual realization* and personal contact, not merely with the astral world, but with God, the Source of all power, wisdom and supply. Thus it was God's power they manifested and which accomplished the marvelous results through them, not psychic power from discarnate mortals.

Man Not A Mortal:

To be practical, just what steps must we take to gain that same realization? We must first of all realize that *we are not mere mortals*, mere human beings, but that we *are spiritual beings* here and now. For there is an individualized Ray of God within each heart, the loving I Am Presence or the Christ-within. All do not have psychic gifts in this life, but all can develop contact with God through seeking to correlate with Him and the Christ within through aspiration and prayer. And progress toward that conscious contact and obedience to His guidance constitutes true spiritual progress.

Meditation:

Therefore, just as some spend many hours each week striving to develop their psychic faculties, so should we seekers for the unfoldment of our spiritual faculties set apart a definite time each day for meditation and prayer for our spiritual unfoldment. Thus, while we fully appreciate the helpfulness, both to our departed friends and to ourselves, of communion with them as we said before, yet it is far more important for us to commune with *in*carnate Spirits than with *dis*carnate spirits, namely, with the Spirit incarnated within ourselves. If they are to progress spiritually, our discarnate friends should also be concerned primarily with their own spiritual conditions rather than the earth conditions around us.

Spiritual Laws:

Now, just as there are psychic laws which we should understand and comply with to contact the astral world, so there are spiritual laws which must be understood and complied with to contact the spiritual world. If we understand these laws we will not have to depend upon the fallible and often mistaken guidance of our departed friends, for that takes away our initiative and self-reliance and makes us learners on them. As we said before, sincere and honest mediums can bring priceless comfort to the bereaved by transmitting messages as nearly right as possible from their loved ones, but we do not have to depend upon them for *spiritual* instruction and personal guidance. We must learn to seek for and depend upon the guidance of the God within, the loving I Am Presence. That guidance *once consciously established* is infallible. This is the great aim of the higher realization: direct guidance by the incarnate Ray of God which is our Real or Spiritual Self.

Cosmic Soul Science:

It is these laws of *spiritual* guidance, as distinct from "spirit guidance," as well as giving a satisfying and scientific explanation of all conditions and problems of manifested existence, that we present in these essays and in the many volumes of teachings which we have received through inspiration.

Spirit Guides:

We know that some spiritualists say that they do not need to study the philosophy of life, as their "guides" tell them all they need to know. But that is a very narrow viewpoint, and intellectually stultifying. The mind needs explanations of the laws and the causes back of all manifested things if it is to have a clear understanding of that which the Spirit is, and that which the spirits reveal.

Contacting Jesus:

No one can be a truly advanced and *spiritual* seeker—as contrasted with a mere spiritist or seeker for phenomena—(many believe in personal survival who are not Spiritualists and who do not live spiritual lives) who does not recognize and strive to correlate with the greatest Spirit that has yet manifested to mankind—the great Master Jesus—and allow His cosmic power to fill him, His cosmic consciousness, to illumine him and His Divine Love to enfold him. We know that many spirit guides say that they have never met or even seen Him. But that is only because they have been content with their activities in the lower realms and have not sent out that aspiration for progress and that love from their hearts which would reach His consciousness, make Him aware of their need and bring His response.

His Name:

Not only is His force present—according to His promise—"Wherever two or three are gathered together in My name," but anyone can tune-in to His consciousness and receive His help at any time if he will use the proper technique of the higher aspiration. For just as your love and mental wireless call for your discarnate friends reaches them and brings its response, just so surely does your love and your spiritual wireless call reach Him and bring His response.

Prayer Measured:

These calls are not mere imagination or metaphysical speculation, but are actual currents of force which can be measured with appropriate instruments. In Washington we have a radionic instrument, using radio tubes, which measures vibrations up to fifty million cycles. With this instrument, in our experiments one day, we took the reading of Mrs. Curtiss' vitality index and found it to be well within the normal range at 37. We then repeated our *Healing Prayer*,[4] and meditated for a few moments on contacting and being filled with the powers invoked. When we felt the answering vibration we took another reading of Mrs. Curtiss' vitality and found that it had risen from 37 to 48 just through the power of that prayer. Then I concentrated the force upon her more directly and her vitality rose still further, up to 60, or *nearly double* the normal reading! So you see that His force is so real that it can be *physically demonstrated* and *scientifically measured*.

---

[4] *Prayers of the O. M. C*, Curtiss, 8.

Response:

Not only do our prayers for our loved ones reach and help them, but all sincere prayers to God reach a Mind that understands and a Heart that is compassionate, loving and *always responsive*. This can be demonstrated to any sincere seeker or even to an entire audience if there are enough present who would like to see a *physical demonstration* of the power of God and *feel it* thrill their physical bodies. It will take only a minute or two, if all present cooperate and assist. Try it just as an experiment, whether you believe in it or not.

Prayer Technique:

First of all, uncross your feet and unclose your hands, for crossing the feet and hands short-circuits you to the forces around you. The right hand is the broadcasting and blessing hand and the hand with which you accomplish in the outer world, but since in this case you do not wish to broadcast the force received but wish to charge yourself with it, place your right hand over the center of your chest (heart), the center of your spiritual forces. The left hand is the receiving hand or the wireless antenna through which you absorb the spiritual forces which your prayers invoke. Therefore, hold the left hand up comfortably, opposite the left shoulder, with the elbow bent and with the fingers spread and the thumb pointing back over the shoulder. While holding this posture repeat the *Prayer for Light*. Remember that it is not only your sincerity, but the intensity of your love and aspiration that sends your current of spiritual force shooting up through the lower realms like a skyrocket to contact the plane to which you aspire. And over this line of light and love you receive the return current from that realm.

Prayer for Light:

First, repeat the *Prayer for Light*. "O Christ! Light Thou within my heart the Flame of Divine Love and

Wisdom, that I may dwell forever in the radiance of Thy countenance and rest in the light of Thy smile."[5]

Visualize:

While still holding this posture, close your eyes just to shut out the outer objective world while you visualize and concentrate your attention upon the downpouring of the Christ-light. Then pray, "O Christ! pour out upon us the radiance of Thy cosmic power! Fill our bodies, our minds and our auras full to overflowing with the blazing light of Thy glory. Let it radiate out in all directions with great dynamic power, overcoming all inertia and spiritual sluggishness, neutralizing all inharmonies and driving out all negative conditions like streams of discolored smoke, until our whole bodies are filled with Thy Divine Light! Let us feel the warmth of its glowing radiance warm our whole being!" (Pause and meditate on this thought until you *feel* a response).

Broadcasting Peace:

Now that you have charged yourself positively with the power of the Christ, *consciously broadcast* it for the help and salvation of the world. Although the foundations of our civilization are threatened with the possibility of a new world war, *it need not happen* if all those who are praying and working for peace and brotherhood will consciously use the power of prayer to neutralize it. Visualize the spiritual power you have invoked going out as a mighty river of radiant golden light which shall engulf the leaders of the nations. See it especially focused on the leaders of the nations, neutralizing their war-thoughts, their national pride of aggression and aggrandizement at the expense of others, and bringing to them a realization that only through love, tolerance, *brotherhood and co-operation* can all the nations of the world prosper and progress and civilization be saved. Thus can the power of the heaven

---

[5] *Prayer of the O. C. M.*, Curtiss, 1.

world, consciously directed and applied, save the world. Amen.

Physical Proof:

We ask all who felt the down-pouring currents of force or the vibrations or the warm current of love thrill their bodies, to make a written record of it. That is a *physical proof* of the objective reality of the forces actually invoked through prayer and co-operation. And once these forces have been felt, you will never forget it the longest day you live. And you can *tune-in to them again* at any time by recalling this moment and visualizing this scene.

Use It:

And now that you have charged yourselves with this Christ-power, and blessed others with it, put it to use in your own lives. Determine to do something every day, *beginning this very day*, to demonstrate your realization of that power. You have been blessed and refreshed and stimulated by it; now radiate it to others. Use every opportunity to say something or do something kind for someone.

Bless Others:

Try to see in everyone the Ray of God he has incarnated to manifest, no matter how much it may be obscured by outer conditions or how little of it he may be manifesting now. If someone has misjudged, criticized or wronged you, do not let his mistake arouse inharmony and resentment in you. Instead, keep your peace and poise within. Forgive him and *send him your blessing* that he may have a greater realization of truth. Then forget the incident. Absolutely refuse to think of it or respond to it all over again.

Stop Criticizing:

No matter how inharmonious the outer personality of your family or associates may be, *stop criticising* and finding fault If your mind is keen enough to see their faults, it is also keen enough to see and comment on their virtues if you will look for them. You can always silently say: "The Christ in me loves the Christ in you." Then feel the warm current of Christ-love flowing out to and enveloping them. Repeat this every time you think of them and note how Divine Love will dissolve all inharmonies, wipe out all antagonism and revolutionize both your life and theirs. Thus will you demonstrate your touch with the heaven world, and make it a practical and dynamic factor in your life.

CHAPTER XII

CHRIST IN THE DAILY LIFE

Refuse Destructive Thoughts:

In these days of tribulation, when the Earth and its humanity are passing through great changes and many dire events, it is not a time to fill our minds with such troubles by enumerating them. Nor is it a time to prophesy dire changes in the near future, even though they may be destined to come. Much less is it a time to select any one person, ruler, nation or condition and pin upon him or it the full responsibility for the deplorable conditions in which the world finds itself.

Blame No One:

It may be that there are those who make themselves channels through which selfish and destructive forces focalize and manifest, yet the evil in the world today is not attributable to any one man, nation or condition, but is the net result of the negative conditions generated by all humanity, who like sheep have strayed from their shepherd and can no longer hear his guiding voice. And without the realization of his guiding presence and loving care they are overcome with fear. In fact, fear is at the bottom of most of the world's troubles today.

Fear Dominates:

Among nations there is fear of invasion, fear of another's greater armaments, fear of another's territorial ambitions and ruthlessness in attaining those ambitions.

In politics there is fear of one party's or policy's being dominated by another. There is fear of one class' exploiting another class. Among individuals there is often fear of sickness, fear of poverty, even fear of old age. All these fears arise from a lack of realization of the Christ and His power, supply and rule. Probably 95% of all man's fears never materialize, so only 5% ever have to be faced.

Attitude Changed:

And once the Power of the Christ is realized, one is so changed that he is no longer the same person who had the fears. This changed attitude toward that which was feared changes the whole course of one's life-stream which seemed to be carrying him toward his fate. So even though the 5% do materialize, they will not have the same effect on him, and his reaction to them will be positive and constructive instead of negative and supine.

Putting on Christ:

But just how are you to learn to utilize the power of the Christ within? What is this Christ within? It is your personalized Ray of the Cosmic Christ. It is the perfect Spiritual Being which is your Real Self. But just how are you to "put on Christ"?.... "for ye are all one in Christ," as St Paul tells us (*Gal.*, iii, 28). This means that you must claim the perfection of the Real or Christ-self within. Then you can enter into the state of Christ-consciousness, the realization of the Christ in you which is waiting for recognition and expression. Then, like Jesus, you must be about your Father's business. How? By doing the work of the Christ in your everyday life and affairs. This work is to *purify, uplift and redeem* the personality, and ultimately all it contacts.

Be Aware of His Presence:

How is this to be done? Fundamentally by consciously striving to let the Christ manifest through you in thought, word and deed—including the tones of your voice—as a result of *your continual awareness* of His presence within, where He observes every action, word and even thought. Allow no one to tell you that you are too imperfect, too faulty, perhaps too sinful, too impure, too weak or too insignificant to permit Him to express through you. For if you waited until you felt worthy, you might never call for His help.

Help Needed Now:

It is now, in your time of trial and temptation, that you need His power to enable you to conquer whatever the Great Law brings to you to be faced. For the Christ within is not something that is abstract or latent. He is a dynamic, expanding, radiating Presence *actively seeking expression* through you. And since this Presence is an individualized Ray of God Himself, He has the whole power of God and the cosmos back of Him, just as every tiniest ray of sunshine has the whole power of the Sun behind it. All that is necessary to give you all the power needed to revolutionize your life is to give Him active expression.

Faith in Yourself:

Therefore, never think of yourself as lacking in power. For you have the whole power of the Cosmic Christ to draw from. But to utilize that Power your first step is to recognize that you already have it within you, just waiting to be called forth into expression. Never admit that persons or things outside yourself have power over you. To do so is to deny the supremacy of the cosmic Power of the Christ within. But to use that Power you must believe in it thoroughly and convincingly. Once you really realize the omnipotence of that Power you can say of all other conditions: "None of these things move me."

Recognize His Power:

Through His Power you can accomplish all that He guides you to do, no matter how impossible it seems at first. Therefore, first recognize the Power, then meditate on it, and then watch for every opportunity to express it. Make yourself positive and dynamic with His Power and you can literally demonstrate the words of our *Morning Prayer:* "I have within me the Power of the Christ. I can conquer all that comes to me today. I am strong enough to bear every trial and to accept every joy, and to say, 'Thy will be done.'"[1] And what joy of triumph and overcoming you experience when you have conquered one fault or failing!

Bodily Purification:

Something of the radiance of the Christ-light and Power will seep through every sincere aspirant, but to let it flow through your various bodies with uninterrupted freedom you must first *purify* them. You must purify them not only of their daily waste, but also of their accumulated acids and toxins by special cleansing methods.[2] Then you must keep them from future accumulations by the use of the right foods, and especially used in the right combinations. If this is understood *and practiced* it will not be necessary to "diet," but merely to use the right combinations and proportions to produce the proper acid-alkaline balance.[1]

Responsive Bodies:

As your bodies are thus *purified* and fed on live and vital foods properly combined, they become *uplifted* in their rates of vibration, become stronger, possess greater endurance and enable you to experience the joy of living. They also become more sensitive and responsive to the Christ impulses from within. Your bodies are thus *re-*

---

[1] *See Prayers of the O. C. M.*, Curtiss, 1.
[2] For details see *Four-Fold Path*, Curtiss.

deemed from their former bondage to sickness and suffering. And what joy of overcoming you experience when you have conquered any inharmony the body may be experiencing! Thus do you do the work of the Christ (purify, uplift and redeem) in your body.

Refuse to Admit:

Secondly, you need to purify your *mind* by purging it of all negative and destructive thoughts. This you can do first by earnestly praying for, and responding to, the mighty flow of peace, harmony and love from the Christ within. Then *keep* the mind pure by *refusing to admit into it* or responding to any thoughts that do not measure up to the ideals you have set for the standard of your life. For all thoughts presented to your mind are not necessarily your thoughts. Many may come from the thought-currents of the community surrounding you. But *if you admit them and dwell upon them* then you make them yours by adoption, and *thereby become responsible* for them.

Gossip:

If bits of gossip, which are usually derogatory, are whispered to you, you should either refuse to listen or you should neutralize them by relating *very positively* something *constructive or complimentary* about the person mentioned. In fact, it is well to *make a definite practice* of always looking for something complimentary or encouraging in all your friends and members of the family. If something unkind is said or done, say or do something kind to offset it and thus shame the doer. And in general, whenever inharmony or criticism arises in the family or social group, if you will start complimenting instead of criticizing, you will *revolutionize, uplift and redeem* the family and group life. Try it and see.

Temptation:

If thoughts appear which tempt you from your duty or your ideals, call upon the Christ within so to flood you with realization of His presence and power that you will lose all sight of the temptation. Hence it will no longer occupy your attention or be a compelling factor in your life.

What You Express:

Since you ultimately express that which you hold in mind, if you long for a vision of heaven you must fix your thoughts on heavenly things frequently, and give them expression. This you can do by holding firmly within and expressing positively your inner peace, harmony and happiness. And as you radiate these forces dynamically and persistently, others will feel your vibrations and respond to them.

An Illustration:

For instance, as we entered a store recently a sales-lady was just concluding with a customer who had evidently caused a great deal of trouble, for the counter was piled with goods she had been shown. She finally flounced away with a disdainful air and some unkind remark about the goods and the service, and the sales-lady turned to us with an impatient and irritated air, almost scowling. Had we responded to her vibrations we would have called impatiently for "service" or "attention." But as we did not wish to take on her negative vibrations we maintained our positive inner harmony and smiled at her instead. Then we remarked: "It takes lots of patience to please some people, doesn't it?" Then she took on our positive and constructive vibration, smiled and replied: "You're telling me?" Thus we dispelled her irritation and cheered her probably for the rest of the day, merely by refusing to respond to her negative vibrations and positively radiating those we chose to manifest.

Keep Positive:

But if you lose your consciousness of the inner peace and harmony of the Christ within, you may become negative and readily take on the inharmonies of outer conditions. Then those things do move you, often very much. When dominated by those outer vibrations you may swear that there is no such state as heavenly bliss. You may react so inharmoniously that life and work seem a veritable hell. But *it is only the character of the thoughts and reactions you permit to manifest through you* that determines whether your life is a hell or a heaven.

Hell or Heaven:

Once realize this and you will discover that you can transform the hell you have produced into the heaven you desire by purifying your thoughts and *refusing to react* to those which are negative. By so doing you raise the vibrations of your mind and send out such powerful, constructive vibrations that you do the work of the Christ (purifying, uplifting and redeeming) in your mental world. And what joy of overcoming you experience when you have consciously conquered one inharmonious thought!

Emotional Control:

Thirdly, having purified, uplifted and redeemed your body and mind, you need to do the same thing for your emotions. First recognize that all the negative emotions, such as anger, hatred, fear, jealousy, envy, etc., *are not your emotions*, but those of the animal through which you have to manifest. Therefore, when you find yourself responding to inharmony or irritation, *refuse to react to them* or they will grow into anger and hatred, and these will poison not only your mind, but your body. Instead say: "O Christ, fill me with Thy peace and poise and power!"

How to Conquer:

If fear assails you, immediately replace it with the courage that is born of the realization of the mighty power of the Christ within. If jealousy arises, replace it with a realization that you have the immortal love of the Christ within, and that therefore the lesser love and admiration of others is not essential to your happiness.

Constructive Emotions:

Then you will respond at once to the constructive realization that "God is Love"; and therefore the Christ within is also love. Hold nothing else in mind. While feeling and responding to His love you cannot be unloving to any one or anything, for you cannot feel love and antagonism at the same time. One neutralizes and excludes the other. If some particular person does not express as much love for you as you think he or she should, you can realize that the Christ within loves you, even if the particular person does not. If you live in His world of love, you are enfolded in that love and it protects you from all else. For it knows no opposition or defeat.

Happiness From Within:

If you are unhappy, realize that your happiness does not depend upon outer conditions or persons, but comes from correlation with your Christ within. When you cease to believe that your joy comes from external things, then you are ready to respond to the joy that your oneness with the Christ gives. That inner joy is constant and unchanging, hence is unaffected by conditions and persons in the outer world. Then you will cease to be swayed like a reed in the wind by conditions outside yourself; for you can still smile even though the Sun is not shining. Your joy and happiness depend upon the degree of your realization of the constant and unfailing inner joy of the Christ. Therefore, *cultivate that realization* by meditating upon it and by constant efforts to express it. Thus you do the work of the Christ in your daily life by *purifying* your emotions, *uplifting* your heart and *redeeming* your life through the power of the indwelling Christ.

> "Life is too brief
> Between the budding and the falling leaf,
> Between the seed-time and the golden sheaf,
>   For hate or spite.
> We have no time for malice and for greed;
> Therefore, with love, make beautiful the deed;
>   Fast speeds the night.
>
> "Life is too swift
> Between the blossom and the white snow's drift,
> Between the silence and the lark's uplift,
>   For bitter words.
> In kindness and gentleness our speech
> Must carry messages of hope, and reach
>   The sweetest chords.
>
> "Life is too great
> Between the infant's and the man's estate,
> Between the clashing of earth's strife and fate,
>   For petty things.
> Lo, we shall yet, who creep with cumbered feet,
> Walk glorious over heaven's golden street,
> Or soar on wings."[3]

---
[3] Author unknown.

INDEX

A

Acorn, 2, 11, 18.
Age, Aquarian, 36, 64; Woman's, 63,72.
All Conquering Love, 103.
Anti-Christ, 39.
Apple, golden, 74.
Apportation, 117.
Aquarians, 65.
Armageddon, 36.
Asceticism, 7.
Aspiration, 122.
Attainment, mount of, 102.

B

Bless others, 124.
Body, must train, 7, 18, 81; purify, 134; Spiritual, 21.
Bread, 70.
Brotherhood, 33.

C

Causation, 2.
Change, 56.
Character, changed, 109.
Childless, 72.
Christ, Cosmic, 22, 55.
Christ in Daily Life, 131.
Clothes, influence of, 43.
Cloud Upon the Mountain, 90, 116.
Colors, 98.
Companionship, 28.
Compassion, 28.
Concepts, fundamental, 2; cosmic, 37.
Consciousness, cosmic, 32; new, 28, 81; God-, 55.
Convict, Love and the, 106.
Co-operation, 29.
Courage and Faith with, 35.
Criticism, stop, 129.
Crowds, 41.
Crusades by women, 67.
Cycles, law of, 19, 63; new, 112.

D

Darkness, 96.
Death, 40.
Demonstration needed, 30.
Denial, 16.
Diakas, 115.
Dimensions, New, 26; fourth, 28.
Druids, 99.

E

Ectoplasm, 96.
Egg, first, 4.
Electrocution, 96.
Emotions, animal, 49, 81-2; human, 106, 137-8.
Empires, colonial, 37.
Etherialization, 92.
Evolution, 2.
Eve, 66.
Existence, Object of, 9, 10, 17, 23.

F

Faculties, psychic, 120.
Faith, 39, 133.
Fears, 82, 131.
Federation, World, 38.
Feminine forces, 33, 66.
Fetish, 115.
Fire, Pillar of, 93.
Food, women prepare, 70.
Frustration, 31.

G

Gossip, 135.
Greatness, 51.
Grindstone, 32.
Growth, 16, 18, 91, 121.
Guides, spirit, 125.

H

Habits, 86, 107.
Happiness, 75, 111, 138.
Heaven, come from, 10, 137.

Heaven World, The, 115.
Herb, before it grew, 3.
Home, earth not our, 6.
Hour-glass, 31.
Hunger, spiritual, 116.

I

I, the little, 102.
Ideals, 54, 62.
Ideas, 58.
Immortality, 6, 123.
Incarnation, necessary, 9; choose, 40.
Intellect, 27.
Inter-dependence, 29.
Invasions, 37.
Invisible, all from the, 1, 9, 90.

J

Jesus, contacting, 125, 132.

K

Karma, 38.

L

Laughter, 78.
Law, cyclic, 63; spiritual, 124.
Levitation, 117.
Life, live, 7; here, temporary, 22; too short, 139.
Linen, 97.
Love, 103; your enemies, 112.

M

Man, not insignificant, 4.
Manifestation, law of, 13.
Materialism, 26.
Materialization, law of, 9, 92.
Matter, spiritualized, 10.
Meditation, 61, 124.
Messages, spirit, 120.
Metals, force of, 97.
Mind, purify, 135.
Mortal, man not a, 5, 123.
Mother, Divine, 65, 103.
Motherhood, 71.

N

Nations, 27.
Nature, laws of, 56.

O

Oak, 11.
Odors, 98.
Old Clothes, 43.
Oneness, 28.
Opinions, of others, 14.

P

Pattern, etheric, 4, 33, 54.
Peace, 40, 128; prayer for, 114.
Phenomena, psychic, 93-8, 117; proof of, 129.
Philosophy of War, 36-8-9.
Pity, self, 49.
Plan and purpose, 2, 5, 37, 54; cosmic, 25; Grand, 33.
Pleiades, 99.
Power, source of, 111, 123.
Prayer for World Peace, 114.
Prayer, measured, 126-7; for Light, 127; why unanswered, 32.
Pre-existence, 3, 5.
Prophecies, 36.
Psychology, 31.
Purgatory, 119.

Q

Quoted.
As You Like It, 79.
Communion with the Spirit World, 95.
Ecclesiastes, 63.
Ephesians, 53.
Exodus, 93.
Four Fold Health, 70, 134.
Genesis, 3.
Greber, Johannes, 95.
Key of Destiny, 63-5.
Key to the Universe, 100.
Message of Aquaria, 63.
Philosophy of War, 36, 114.
Poems, 42, 88, 139.
Prayers, 114, 126-7, 134.
Realms of the Living Dead, 52, 93, 118.
St. John, 3, 10.
Secret Doctrine, The, 9.
Thirty Years Among the Dead, 119.

Truth About Evolution and the Bible, 66.
Voice of Isis, The, 94.

R

Radiation, law of, 80, 105, 136.
Reincarnation, 19.
Resurrection, 20.
Rib, 66.
Righteousness, Sun of, 14, 21.

S

Sacrifice, 31.
Saints, 118.
Science, Cosmic Soul, 90, 125.
Self, Spiritual, 8, 102.
Sensitiveness, 15.
Ship-acquaintances, 48.
Skotographs, 80.
Slavery, 37.
Smile, Smile, Smile, 75; poem, 88.
Son, 21.
Soul, individualized, 8.
Spring, 11, 14.
Standards, four, 24.
Suffering, 32.
Survival, personal, 115, 118.

T

Teleplasm, 96.
Temptations, 136.
Tennyson, quoted, 38.

Test all, 24.
Thought, laws of, 60, 119.
Thoughts, old, 45.
Thunder, 100.
Trials, 15.
Tyrants, 30.

U

Unity, of mankind, 28.
Unseen, all from the, 1, 9, 90.
Uranus, 64.

V

Victory, poem, 42.
Vision of Convict, 106.
Visualize, 128.
Voice, independent, 95-8-9, 102.
Voodoo, 115.

W

Water, 65, 104.
Wig, judges, 101.
Will, not your own, 10, 17; Father's, 17.
Woman's Age, 63-8-9-, 73; duty, 33.
World, The Heaven, 115.

Y

Youth, 72.

www.ingramcontent.com/pod-product-compliance
Lightning Source LLC
Chambersburg PA
CBHW071507040426
42444CB00008B/1529